Healthy Living Kitchen™

A Recipe for Life

A Recipe
for
Life

The University of Tennesee Medical Center

Jane Kelly, RN, BSN, CWPC, **Janet Seiber**, RD, LDN, CDE,
Mark McKinney, Senior Executive Chef

Nutritional Analysis

Nutritional analysis is calculated for each recipe in this cookbook. It is for reference only and should not be considered exact as nutritional information may vary by cooking methods, brand of ingredients, variations in measurements, serving sizes, etc. Consult your dietitian or physician for your exact nutritional needs.

ISBN 978-1-105-06295-7

Dedication

This book is dedicated to all the participants of the Healthy Living Kitchen, especially the loyal cooking class participants who have inspired this book's creation.

Table of Contents

THE UNIVERSITY OF TENNESSEE
MEDICAL CENTER

Wisdom for Your Life.

To serve through healing, education, and discovery

With a three-fold mission of healing, education, and discovery, The University of Tennessee Medical Center holds unique prominence. As the region's only academic medical center and Level I trauma center, The University of Tennessee Medical Center serves as a major referral center for East Tennessee, Southeast Kentucky, and Western North Carolina. The 581-bed hospital is home to the region's only dedicated Heart Hospital, Magnet® recognized facility, adult and pediatric transplant center, and the region's first certified primary stroke center.

The University of Tennessee Medical Center established the Healthy Living Kitchen™ program in 2006 in response to our region's need for simple, healthy, and delicious recipes. East Tennesseans have been raised on traditional southern cooking. Although very tasty, it is often high in fat and carbohydrates. As a result of this type of diet, along with lack of physical activity, our obesity and diabetes rates are some of the highest in the country.

The Healthy Living Kitchen offers a multidisciplinary approach to cooking. Our team consists of a registered dietitian, cardiac nurse specialist, and executive chef who provide expertise in nutrition and preventative health education along with culinary skills.

The Healthy Living Kitchen teaches simple ways to use fresh ingredients and modify recipes for our fast-paced lives. Cooking with fresh foods, such as fruits, vegetables, whole grains, and lean meats, can prevent and manage many diseases including cardiovascular disease, diabetes, and celiac disease. Prevention of these diseases also includes weight management, stress management, and physical activity.

The Healthy Living Kitchen provides individuals with the knowledge and skills needed to improve nutritional choices and live a healthier lifestyle by offering cooking classes, grocery shopping tours, and interactive presentations.

For more information on the Healthy Living Kitchen program visit
www.utmedicalcenter.org/healthylivingkitchen.

Healthy Living Kitchen Team

(pictured from left to right: Janet Seiber, Mark McKinney, Jane Kelly)

Mark McKinney, Senior Executive Chef

Mark McKinney is the senior executive chef at The University of Tennessee Medical Center. As the chef for the Healthy Living Kitchen, he provides lessons on cooking tips, knife skills, and food presentation that give class participants the skills and confidence for healthy cooking. His recipes fit into many healthy eating plans because they are simple, fresh, and delicious.

Chef McKinney is a culinary arts graduate of Johnson and Wales University. He has worked at Magnolias and The Woodlands in South Carolina and several local restaurants, including The Inn at Blackberry Farm, Little City Bistro, and as executive sous chef at Bravo. He is on the faculty at the University of Tennessee teaching cooking classes through the personal and professional development department. Chef McKinney helped develop the room service program at M.D. Anderson Cancer Center in Houston.

Jane Kelly, RN, BSN, CWPC

Jane Kelly, RN, BSN, CWPC, is a cardiac nurse specialist for the Healthy Living Kitchen and was the inspiration for the development of the program. While counseling patients on making preventative lifestyle changes, she identified a need for healthy cooking classes to teach individuals how to make modifications to their diet and recipes. As the nurse educator for the Healthy Living Kitchen, she finds new and creative ways for individuals to practice wellness. She is also a community speaker on diabetes, wellness, and cardiovascular disease.

Kelly graduated from the University of Tennessee with a bachelor of nursing. Jane is a certified wellness program coordinator through the National Wellness Institute. She is also a certified lifestyle counselor with 25 years of nursing experience in cardiac nursing and wellness. Kelly has been very active in the American Heart Association as a CPR instructor, Heart Walk captain, and was a panel speaker for the 2008 Go Red Luncheon. Kelly was the 2009 recipient of the Tennessee Dietetic Association IRIS Award. She is a member of the Preventive Cardiology Nurses Association.

Janet Seiber, RD, LDN, CDE

Janet Seiber, RD, LDN, CDE, has been with the Healthy Living Kitchen program since its inception in 2006. As the Healthy Living Kitchen's registered dietitian, she gives participants practical advice about the link between nutrition and health. She shows attendees how to improve nutritional choices by learning how to read food labels, plan menus, modify recipes, and follow current diet guidelines. She believes that small changes with eating habits and food selection make a big impact on overall health and wellness.

Seiber holds a bachelor of science degree in nutrition from the University of Tennessee and completed a dietetic internship with Vanderbilt University Medical Center. She is a registered dietitian and is licensed in the state of Tennessee as a dietitian/nutritionist, and a certified diabetes educator. Seiber has been with UT Medical Center since 2002 providing medical nutrition therapy with an emphasis on cardiovascular disease, diabetes, and weight management for inpatient, outpatient, and corporate areas. She is a member of the Academy of Nutrition and Dietetics.

Acknowledgements from
The Healthy Living Kitchen Team

We would like to thank The University of Tennessee Medical Center Senior Leadership Team, specifically Norman Majors, chief administrative officer, for encouraging the Healthy Living Kitchen team to create a cookbook that will serve as a guide for individuals in their journey towards better health.

Teresa Levey, vice president of the Heart Lung Vascular Institute, for her support and leadership of the Healthy Living Kitchen. Through her leadership, the Healthy Living Kitchen program was created to offer nutritional guidance for improving the health of individuals.

Morrison Healthcare and UT Medical Center Department of Nutrition and Food Services, specifically Virginia Turner, clinical nutrition manager and long time advocate of the Healthy Living Kitchen program.

Many colleagues offered their expertise, time, and enthusiasm to this project. We would like to thank the following hospital departments and others for their assistance and guidance in the development of this cookbook: Clinical Nutrition, Marketing, Healthcare Coordination, Employee Fitness, Hospital Auxiliary, and the Office of Development.

Network Development, especially Rhonda McAnally and Shannon Reynolds for supporting the development of this cookbook.

Food City and K-VA-T Food Stores, Inc. for sponsoring the Healthy Living Kitchen program and for their assistance in the promotion of health and wellness in the community. This cookbook would not have been possible without their generous support.

ASEN Marketing & Advertising for the photography shown in this book. Thank you for capturing the essence of our delicious recipes.

A special thank you to Cara Hedges and Kori Higgins, dietetic students, for the many hours spent researching the nutritional education content included in this cookbook.

Thank you to the additional chefs that donated their time and culinary talents to create healthy and delicious recipes with the Healthy Living Kitchen. Selected recipes are provided by the following:

Monty Lowans served as the executive chef for The University of Tennessee Medical Center from 2006–2008 and helped develop the Healthy Living Kitchen program. His creativity and enthusiasm for food inspired many of the recipes included in this cookbook. Monty's recipes, Asian Tuna Wrap and Chipotle Portobello Sandwich, were featured in the article *Tailgating Lite* in *Today's Diet and Nutrition* magazine.

Chef Walter Lambert, known as the beloved chef of WVLT-TV, the CBS affiliate in Knoxville, joined the Healthy Living Kitchen team for the cooking classes

Spring Treats and Culinary Workshop in 2011. Having lost more than 90 pounds by following a healthy eating and weight loss program at The University of Tennessee Medical Center, Chef Walter is a living example of how diet and exercise can improve diabetes, high blood pressure, and weight management.

Janet McKenzie Prince, career journalist and photographer, was diagnosed with celiac disease in 2000. She is a community advocate for celiac disease. Janet has been a featured guest speaker and has shared several gluten-free recipes with our gluten-free classes. It is her passion to promote awareness through her book *My Gluten-Free Knoxville*.

John Day of Morrison's Healthcare served as interim chef for our 2008 holiday cooking class.

Lastly, we would like to thank our families for their support and for sampling the many modified recipes we tried until we got it right!

Nutrition
and
Lifestyle Management

Nutrition Planning

Basic nutrition skills help you make informed choices about your diet. Knowing how to read a food label and learning healthy food options in each food group gives you the tools to make healthy choices. Many times simply being more aware of food choices helps to improve your eating habits. Planning ahead makes it easier to cook nutritious meals at home.

Food Labels

Whether you follow a special diet or simply want to eat healthy, the food label provides information that helps make proper food choices.

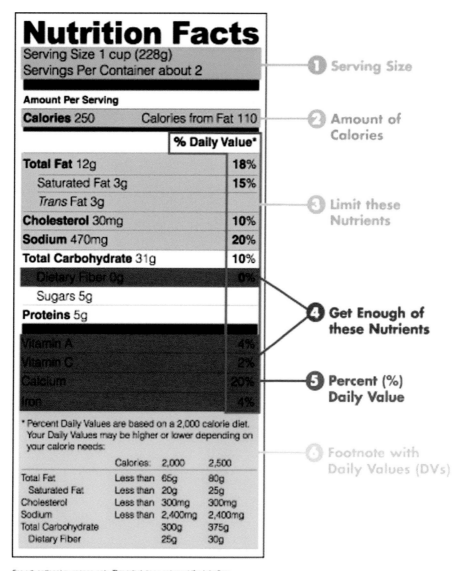

Serving Size: The first place to look when reading the label is the serving size. There may be more than one serving per container. Make sure to adjust the other numbers when eating a serving size different than the package.

Calories: Calories are the amount of energy the food provides. If a product states "sugar-free" or "fat-free", make sure it has fewer calories.

Fats and Cholesterol: To reduce blood cholesterol levels, it is more important to check saturated fat and trans fat than cholesterol amounts in food. Eat less than 7% calories from saturated fat and avoid trans fats as much as possible.

Sodium: Eating less than 2400 mg sodium per day helps prevent high blood pressure. Foods with more than 350 mg sodium per serving are high sodium food choices.

Carbohydrates: Fiber and sugar are included in the total carbohydrate amount. Aim for at least 25 grams of fiber per day. Choose grain products with at least 3 grams fiber per serving. Fruits, vegetables, and beans are other sources of fiber. Compare products to reduce the amount of sugar in the diet.

Protein: Choose sources of protein that are low in saturated fat like lean meat and low-fat dairy products.

The % Daily Value: The percentages are based on a 2000-calorie diet and can help determine if a food is high or low in a nutrient. If it has 5% or less, it is a low source. If it has 20% or more, it is a high source.

Ingredient List: Items on the list of ingredients are in order of prominence.

Healthy Food Choices Using MyPlate

My plate is a graphic designed to help remind us to keep portions in check and eat a balanced diet. In our classes, we use a 9-inch plate to help control portion sizes.

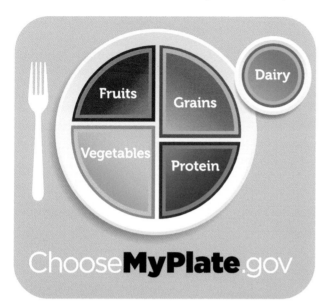

Find your balance between food and physical activity, know the limits on fats, sugars and salt (sodium).

Grains	Vegetables	Fruits	Dairy	Protein
Make half your grains whole	**Vary your veggies**	**Focus on fruits**	**Get your calcium-rich foods**	**Go lean with protein**
Eat at least 3 oz. of whole-grain cereals, breads,crackers, rice or pasta every day	Eat more dark-green veggies like broccoli, spinach and other dark leafy greens	Eat a variety of fruit	Go low-fat or fat-free	Choose low-fat or lean meats and poultry
1 oz. is about 1 slice of bread, about 1 cup of breakfast cereal, or ½ cup of cooked rice, cereal or pasta	Eat more orange vegetables like carrots and sweet potatoes	Choose fresh, frozen, canned or dried fruit	If you don't or can't consume milk, choose lactose-free products or other calcium sources such as fortified foods and beverages	Bake it, broil it, or grill it
	Eat more dry beans and peas like pinto beans, kidney beans and lentils	Go easy on fruit juices		Vary your protein routine–choose more fish, beans, peas, nuts and seeds

For a 2,000-calorie diet, you need the amounts below from each food group.
To find the amounts that are right for you, go to ChooseMyPlate.gov

Eat 6 oz. every day	Eat 2½ cups every day	Eat 2 cups every day	Get 3 cups every day; for kids aged 2 to 8, it's 2	Eat 5½ oz. every day

Grocery Shopping Tips

Grains	Vegetables	Fruit	Dairy	Meat

Whole Grain Choices:
• Whole Wheat
  • bread
  • English muffins
  • tortillas
  • pasta
• brown rice
• popcorn
• oatmeal
• barley
 	
• "100% whole wheat" should be first ingredient
 	
• Choose "whole wheat" instead of "multi-grain"
 	
• Choose foods with at least 3 grams of fiber per serving
	Best Picks:
	• fresh
	• frozen, no sauce
	• no added salt canned
	
	• Choose colorful vegetables like:
	  • bell peppers
	  • broccoli
	  • eggplant
	  • pumpkin
	  • spinach
	  • tomatoes
	
	• Include beans like pinto, black, kidney and garbanzo
	
	• Limit starchy vegetables
	
	• Try precut and prewashed vegetables
		Healthy buys:
		• fresh
		• frozen
		• dried
		• canned, no added sugar
		
		• Include colorful fruits like:
		  • blueberries
		  • raspberries
		  • strawberries
		  • plums
		  • oranges
		  • cantaloupe
		
		• Limit fruit juice to 1 cup of 100% juice per day
		
		• Limit dried fruit to ¼ cup per day
			Select:
			• skim or 1% milk
			• yogurt, light or reduced fat
			• cheese, fat-free or reduced fat
			• cream cheese, fat-free
			• sour cream, fat-free
			• soy milk, reduced fat
			• cottage cheese, fat-free
			• evaporated skim milk
			
			• Natural cheeses are better than processed cheeses
				Go for:
				• Chicken or turkey breast, skinless
				• round or loin cuts of beef and pork
				• fish & shellfish (not fried)
				• Canadian bacon
				• sandwich meats
				• tofu
				• eggs (omega 3)
				
				• Strive to eat fish at least 2 times per week
				
				• salmon, trout, herring, mackerel and tuna contain heart-healthy omega-3 fats

Snacks	Oils & Fats
• Ideas: frozen yogurt, sorbet, light ice cream, sugar-free popsicles, snack size popcorn, fresh fruit, cereal bars, raw vegetables, ginger snaps, pretzels, melba toast, rice cakes and 100 calorie packs • Portion control is important with snacking • "Sugar-free" and "Fat-free" do not mean the product is low in carbohydrates or calories • Make snacks less than 200 calories per serving • Pre-portion snacks with sandwich bags when you get home from the store	• Best oils: canola, olive, corn, safflower, sunflower and other liquid vegetable oils • Healthiest spread choices: tub margarine (without trans fat) or light butter • Other fats: light/fat-free mayonnaise, light/fat-free salad dressing, vinaigrette salad dressing, avocado and olives • Unsalted nuts and seeds are healthy fats (try to incorporate one serving 3-5 times per week): -walnuts, pecans, almonds or peanuts (¼ cup) -flaxseed, pumpkin, or sunflower seeds (2 Tablespoons) -natural peanut or almond butter (2 Tablespoons)

Meal Planning

Planning ahead saves *time and money* and can increase nutritional value. Almost always, meals prepared at home have less fat and sodium than restaurant meals. The key is making sure the kitchen is stocked with nutritious foods. Set aside time to plan meals and make grocery lists. Think about how many days it benefits you to plan ahead. Some plan weekly, while others plan for fewer days. Select recipes. Make a shopping list. Put the plan into action. This is an ongoing process that can be revised to fit your needs.

Healthy Food Choices: Aim for recommended servings of whole grains, vegetables, fruits, lean meats or vegetarian protein sources, and low-fat dairy. Picture your plate as ¼ starch, ¼ meat and ½ fruits and vegetables. Add extra vegetables to one-pot meals, casseroles, salads, sandwiches, and pasta dishes.

Make a Colorful Plate: A variety of colors will increase the nutrient content of meals, plus it will look more appetizing.

Eat a Variety of Foods: A balanced diet is achieved by consuming a variety of foods. The same meal over and over can get boring. Try different types of meals: poultry, red meat (lean cuts), fish, one-dish meals (pasta or stir-fry), seasonal meal (entrée salad or stew), and meatless meals.

Recipe Review: Make healthy substitutions to your own recipes. Search for new, healthy recipes. Avoid recipes with too many ingredients. Look for fresh ingredients that provide more fiber and less sodium and fat.

Money-saving Tips: Choose fruits and vegetables that are in season. They typically cost less. When meats are on sale at the store buy more and freeze for later use.

What about Busy Schedules? Plan a slow-cooker meal. Arrange to cook once then use leftovers for next night's meal. Fix and freeze meals to have healthy food in-house. A few minutes of planning helps prevent stressful mealtimes.

Nutrition and Heart Disease

The Healthy Living Kitchen began with the mission to promote a heart-healthy lifestyle that reduces the risk for cardiovascular disease because heart disease is still the number one killer for both women and men. Cardiovascular disease includes blocked arteries, heart attack, stroke, heart valve problems, irregular heartbeat, and heart failure. There are many risk factors for developing heart disease.

Risk factors that can be controlled include:

- High blood cholesterol
- High blood pressure
- Overweight or obese
- Inactivity
- High blood sugar
- Tobacco use

Risk factors that cannot be controlled include:

- Family history
- Genetics
- Age

The more risk factors you have, the greater your chances of developing heart disease. The Healthy Living Kitchen provides healthy recipes and life skills to help reduce the risk factors for heart disease that can be controlled.

Nutrition and lifestyle advice can enhance medication and medical management. The nutrition information in this book is not meant to diagnose or treat any illness. If you have been diagnosed with a heart condition, including high blood pressure, you should follow your doctor's advice. Medications are often prescribed to control high cholesterol and blood pressure. If you have heart disease you should always consult with your physician before making any major diet and lifestyle changes.

Nutrition Tips to Control Cholesterol Levels

Cholesterol is a substance made by the body and needed for cells, immune system, and food digestion. Too much cholesterol will increase your risk for heart disease. There are two different types of cholesterol that effect heart disease risk differently.

LDL cholesterol (bad cholesterol) is the type that can cause plaque to form in the arteries that may block blood flow from the heart. Lowering levels of LDL cholesterol can reduce risk for heart disease. To reduce LDL levels, eat less saturated fat (<7% calories from saturated fat), avoid trans fat (hydrogenated oils), and eat more fiber.

HDL cholesterol (good cholesterol) is the type that removes harmful, artery clogging cholesterol from the bloodstream. Optimal levels of HDL cholesterol will reduce risk for heart disease. You can raise good cholesterol by exercising on a regular basis and quitting smoking. Dietary changes to raise HDL levels include eating more unsaturated fats like fish oil, nuts, and seeds.

Triglycerides are a type of fat found in the blood. Triglycerides are made from the food we eat, specifically fat and carbohydrates the body does not use immediately for energy. High levels of triglycerides can raise the risk of developing heart disease and are linked to other risk factors like diabetes, high blood pressure, and obesity. To lower triglycerides, minimize extra carbohydrates from sources like sugar, alcohol, and large portions of starchy foods. Increase omega-3 fatty acid intake, especially from fatty fish. Other lifestyle measures to lower triglycerides include losing weight and exercising on a regular basis.

Recommended Levels	
Total Cholesterol mg/dL	< 200
LDL Cholesterol mg/dL	< 130 if no risk factors < 100 if 2 or more risk factors < 70 if heart disease
HDL Cholesterol mg/dL	> 40 men > 50 women
Triglycerides mg/dL	< 150

Use the following to improve total cholesterol and LDL levels

Eat Less Saturated Fat: Eat less than 7% calories from saturated fat per day (for example, 16 grams saturated fat when eating a 2000 calorie diet).

- Bake, grill, or broil foods; avoid fried foods; and eat 5–6 ounces lean meat, poultry, or fish per day.

- Try skinless chicken/turkey breast, round or loin cuts of beef/pork, or fish/shellfish.

- Eat 2–3 servings "cold water" fish (e.g., tuna, salmon, mackerel, halibut, swordfish, sardines, lake trout) per week. 1 serving = 3 ounces.

- Choose low fat dairy products and limit egg yolks to 3 per week.

- Instead of butter, use tub margarine with no trans fat or whipped butter.

Eat More Fiber: Include 25–35 grams of dietary fiber per day. Increase fiber intake slowly to avoid digestive problems.

- Choose whole wheat bread, pasta, crackers, and cereals

- Whole grain choices: oatmeal, brown rice, barley, whole wheat couscous, quinoa.

- Increase intake of beans such as lentils, edamame, black-eyed peas, pinto, black, garbanzo, and kidney beans.

- Eat 5 servings or more of fruits and vegetables each day.

Use the following to improve HDL levels

Eat More Unsaturated Fats:

- Eat fish 3 times per week.

- Use small to moderate amounts of olive oil or canola oil.

- Include one daily: 2 tablespoons of ground flaxseed, 1 tablespoon flaxseed oil, 2–3 tablespoons of walnuts, almonds, or natural peanut butter per day.

Use the following to improve triglyceride levels

Minimize "Extras" in Diet:

- Decrease all refined sugar in diet, including soda, fruit juice, fat-free desserts, candy, cakes, and cookies.

- Decrease all "white flour" products, such as white bread, pasta, crackers, rice, pretzels, corn, potatoes, and many cereals.

- Limit simple sugar intake to 1–2 servings per week. 1 serving = 100 calories.

- Eat less saturated fat and include sources of unsaturated fats.

- Avoid alcohol.

- Keep food portions and overall calories in balance to promote weight management.

Types of Fat

Saturated Fat: A type of fat that can raise bad cholesterol levels. It is solid at room temperature. Sources include animal products such as meat, milk, and cheese. It is also found in tropical oils.

Monounsaturated Fat: This fat may help lower bad cholesterol and raise good cholesterol in the body. It is in liquid vegetable oils, such as canola, olive, and peanut oils. Other food sources include avocados and olives.

Polyunsaturated Fat: This fat is found in other liquid vegetable oils such as safflower, sunflower, sesame, soybean, and corn oils. Polyunsaturated fat is also the main fat found in seafood. Eating polyunsaturated fat in place of saturated fat may lower LDL cholesterol. Omega-3 fatty acids are a type of polyunsaturated fat that may reduce the risk of heart disease. Ground flaxseed, flaxseed oil, nuts, and seeds also have omega-3 fatty acids.

Trans Fat: Hydrogenated oil is another term for trans fat. Trans fat can raise your bad cholesterol, so avoid trans fat completely if possible. It is found in stick margarine and some processed foods. It is listed on the food label, but if the product has less than .5 gram trans fat, it is sometimes rounded down to zero. Check ingredient lists for hydrogenated oils—this means trans fat is a part of the food.

The Mediterranean Diet

The Healthy Living Kitchen uses the Mediterranean diet as inspiration for creating recipes and menus. The Mediterranean diet is based on the lifestyle of people living in countries bordering the Mediterranean Sea, including Spain, Italy, France, Greece, and countries of Northern Africa. A Mediterranean eating pattern emphasizes fruits and vegetables; healthy fats such as olive oil and avocados; heart-healthy nuts such as almonds and walnuts; whole grains; cold water fish high in omega-3 fatty acids; low fat or fat free dairy products, especially yogurt; and the moderate consumption of red wine or purple grape juice. There is an emphasis on fish as the preferred protein source, reducing the amount of red meat. A healthy dose of regular physical activity also is a vital component of the Mediterranean lifestyle.

There are several benefits associated with the Mediterranean diet. A major difference in this pattern of eating and a typical heart-healthy diet is the higher percentage of total fat allowed. The Mediterranean diet can be as high as 40% of calories from fat, compared to 30% recommended by most heart-healthy eating plans, but the type of fat in the diet makes a big difference in terms of heart health. Studies have shown those eating a Mediterranean diet increases blood levels of omega-3 fatty acids, vitamins C and E, and decreased markers of inflammation. Research also has shown that adherence to this eating pattern can prevent a second occurrence of a heart attack and reduce your overall risk of death from heart disease. An overall risk of cancer also was observed in persons eating a Mediterranean diet. The component that helps cancer prevention was not determined, but the emphasis on intake of high fiber and antioxidant-rich whole grains, fruits, and vegetables are likely candidates.

The emphasis on healthy fats plays a significant role in the Mediterranean diet's health benefits. Omega-3 fatty acids are known to be associated with reduced inflammation. Improving the ratio of omega-3 fatty acids to omega-6 fatty acids affects the inflammatory processes in our bodies. Many chronic diseases, including heart disease and cancer, are now thought to be caused at least partly by chronic inflammation. The emphasis on intake of antioxidant rich fruits and vegetables, as well as red wine, also help fight inflammation.

Mediterranean Diet Pyramid

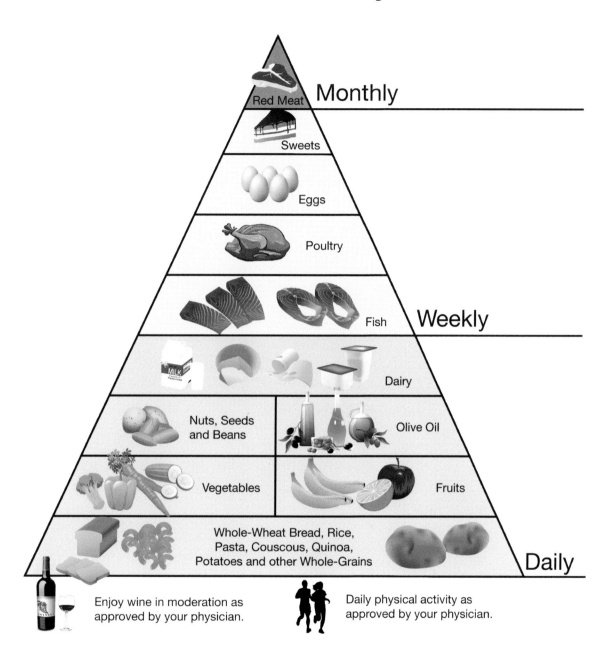

Monthly

Red Meat

Sweets

Eggs

Poultry

Fish   Weekly

Dairy

Nuts, Seeds and Beans   Olive Oil

Vegetables   Fruits

Whole-Wheat Bread, Rice, Pasta, Couscous, Quinoa, Potatoes and other Whole-Grains   Daily

Enjoy wine in moderation as approved by your physician.

Daily physical activity as approved by your physician.

Nutrition Tips To Control High Blood Pressure

Blood pressure is the force of blood pushing against artery walls going through your body. The top number, systolic, is the pressure when the heart squeezes to pump blood to the body. The bottom number, diastolic, is the pressure when the heart is resting between beats. A normal blood pressure goal is less than 120/80. Hypertension is the medical term for high blood pressure. Over time, high blood pressure raises risk for developing heart disease, especially heart attack and heart failure. High blood pressure affects the entire body. It is the leading cause of stroke and major cause of kidney disease. Hypertension is known as the "silent killer" because there are often no symptoms as it is damaging the body over time. It is very important to know your blood pressure number and check it often.

Blood Pressure	
Normal	Less than 120 and less than 80
At Risk for High Blood Pressure	120–139 / 80–89
High Blood Pressure	140 or higher or 90 or higher

There are many ways to prevent and control high blood pressure. Lifestyle strategies include physical activity, managing weight and stress, limiting alcohol, and eating a healthy diet that has less sodium. An eating plan proven to lower blood pressure is the DASH diet (Dietary Approaches to Stop Hypertension).

Ways to Reduce Sodium in Your Diet

Eat less than 2400 mg sodium per day, which is equivalent to one teaspoon of salt. Your physician may recommend reducing sodium to 1500 mg per day to control blood pressure. The daily sodium amount includes table salt as well as sodium already in the food. In fact, most of the sodium in our diets comes from processed foods versus added salt at the table.

- Choose fresh foods; they are naturally lower in sodium.

- Add less salt when cooking and be very careful when adding any salt at the table.

- If you use a salt shaker, make a new habit to taste food first. If it needs more flavor use salt-free seasonings, like pepper, as a substitute.

- Enhance flavor by using herbs, spices, vinegars, citrus, and salt-free seasoning blends.

- It is essential to read the food label when monitoring for sodium intake. A food that has more than 350 mg sodium per serving is a high sodium choice.

- Processed foods that may be high in sodium include:
  - Many fast food items: burgers, pizza, burritos, hot dogs
  - Condiments: pickles, soy sauce, barbecue sauce
  - Pre-packed frozen foods: pot pies, rice/pasta mixes, frozen dinners
  - Canned foods: soups, baked beans, meats

The D.A.S.H. Diet

Food Group	Servings Per Day	Serving Size
Grains	6 to 8 servings	1 slice of bread ½ cup cereal, rice, or pasta Make whole-grain, high fiber choices
Vegetables	4 to 5 servings	1 cup of raw leafy vegetables ½ cup of raw or cooked vegetables ½ cup vegetable juice
Fruits	4 to 5 servings	1 medium-sized piece of fruit ½ cup fresh or canned fruit ¼ cup dried fruit ½ cup fruit juice
Low-fat and fat-free milk and milk products	2 to 3 servings	1 cup milk 1 cup yogurt 1½ ounces cheese
Lean meat, poultry, fish	5 to 6 servings	A serving is 1 ounce chicken or turkey breast Round or loin cuts of beef and pork Fish that is not deep-fried
Beans, nuts, seeds	4 to 5 servings a week	¼ cup nuts 2 tablespoons seeds ½ cup cooked dried beans or peas
Fats and oils	2 to 3 servings	1 teaspoon tub margarine or oil 1 tablespoon mayonnaise 2 tablespoons salad dressing
Sweets and added sugars	5 servings a week or less	1 tablespoon sugar ½ cup frozen yogurt 1 cup of lemonade

The DASH eating plan emphasizes fruits, vegetables, and whole grain servings along with fat-free dairy products, fish, chicken and turkey breast, beans, seeds, and nuts. It limits sugar, fat, and salt, and has less red meat than the typical American diet. The DASH diet is heart healthy since it is lower in saturated fat, trans fat, and cholesterol. It has plenty of potassium, magnesium, and calcium, which are associated with lowering blood pressure when eaten from food sources.

Nutrition and Diabetes

Type-2 diabetes is the most common type of diabetes. It occurs when the body becomes resistant to insulin and blood glucose (blood sugar) is not processed properly. When insulin is not working correctly glucose does not provide energy for the body's cells. Glucose stays in the blood stream in higher amounts than usual, and over time health problems may develop.

If you have diabetes, the treatment goal is to control blood glucose in order to prevent long-term complications of uncontrolled blood sugar such as heart disease and stroke. Your physician should provide goals for blood glucose readings and other treatments to stay healthy.

Nutrition and lifestyle changes are an essential component of diabetes management. Foods that contain carbohydrate turn into glucose. It is not advisable to eliminate carbohydrate foods because we need them for energy and they are sources of fiber, vitamins, and minerals. The key is controlling the portions of carbohydrate foods.

Carbohydrate food sources:

- Starches: bread, cereal, rice, pasta, crackers
- Starchy vegetables: potatoes, corn, peas, dried beans
- Fruit
- Milk and yogurt
- Sweets: soft drinks, cake, pie, candy, cookies, ice cream

Keep carbohydrate portions in check by measuring food portions, reading food labels and learning which foods contain carbohydrate. Exchange lists provide information on carbohydrate foods and serving sizes. Food labels give amounts of total carbohydrate for the serving size listed on the package. One carbohydrate serving is equal to 15 grams total carbohydrate on the food label. All recipes in this cookbook give the amount of carbohydrates in grams. When selecting recipes, use the carbohydrate amount to determine how it fits into your meal plan.

The amount of carbohydrate to be included with each meal and snack varies with each person. No one meal plan fits everyone. Gender, age, activity level, diabetes medications, and personal preferences influence every meal plan. A typical meal size is 3–4 carbohydrate servings or 45–60 grams total carbohydrate and a typical snack size is 1–2 carbohydrate servings or 15–30 grams total carbohydrate.

Meal timing and food amounts may need to be adjusted with certain diabetes medications or insulin. For most people, eating about the same amount of carbohydrate at each meal and eating meals about the same time each day can help regulate blood glucose levels. It is recommended to space meals 4–5 hours apart. For example, breakfast at 7:30 am, lunch at noon, snack at 4:00 pm, and dinner at 6:30 pm. Spacing your meals this way can also help control your appetite by not letting you get too hungry.

A registered dietitian can assist with creating an individualized meal plan for you. Ask your doctor about a referral to a registered dietitian. If you have diabetes, you are at an increased risk for developing heart disease. Choose foods that control blood cholesterol levels so the risk of developing heart disease is reduced. This includes choosing lean meats, low-fat dairy products, and high fiber foods such as whole grains, fruits, and vegetables. Remember, all the Healthy Living Kitchen recipes in this book are created to promote a healthy heart.

Millions of Americans are at risk for developing diabetes. Risk factors include age, obesity, inactivity, and family history. If your fasting blood glucose level is more than 100 mg/dl, or your doctor has ever mentioned prediabetes, it is time to take action to prevent the development of diabetes. Losing weight, eating healthy, and most importantly, increasing physical activity will help you to prevent diabetes.

If you are overweight, even a 5% weight loss can help your body with better blood sugar control. The amount of calories you eat and physical activity affects your weight. Measuring foods and reading food labels help to control portion sizes and calorie intake. Increase your activity level to burn more calories. Consult with your doctor before starting a strenuous exercise program. Read on for more information on exercise and weight management.

Nutrition and Celiac Disease

Celiac disease is a digestive disorder where the intestines cannot tolerate gluten, a protein in wheat, barley, and rye. Once exposed to products containing gluten, an immune response occurs by damaging the lining of the intestines. Without healthy absorption of food a person eventually becomes malnourished. The symptoms of celiac disease differ in each person and some have no outward effects at all. This disease often goes undiagnosed with symptoms such as abdominal pain, gas, bloating, diarrhea, nausea, anemia, unexplained weight loss and many other symptoms.

An increasing number of people have celiac disease. A recent study revealed that 1 in 133 Americans have the disease. Anyone from childhood to the elderly can develop celiac as it is a genetic disorder. It often goes undiagnosed for years, commonly over a decade for adults.

The main treatment for celiac disease is a gluten-free diet. This means avoiding any gluten-containing products. Switching to a gluten-free diet before a diagnosis of celiac disease can affect testing results. Celiac disease is diagnosed with blood testing and confirmed with an intestinal biopsy. You should always discuss a gluten-free diet change with your physician or dietitian. Once gluten-free, symptoms usually improve, but it may take many months for the small intestine to fully heal and improve nutrient absorption.

A gluten-free diet avoids most grains, pasta, cereals, and many processed foods. Use instead grain products made from these types of flour: potato, rice, soy, quinoa, buckwheat, amaranth, or bean flour. Other starchy foods to include are rice, corn, potatoes, sweet potatoes, peas, beans, and quinoa. Many food additives also contain gluten.

Staples of the gluten-free diet include:

- Corn or rice cereals made without wheat or barley malt

- Potatoes, rice, corn, beans

- Fruits and vegetables

- Meat, poultry, and fish (not breaded or made with regular gravies)

- Dairy products

- Gluten-free oats (may be okay for some people with celiac disease, but work closely with your doctor or dietitian)

Changing to a gluten-free diet can be challenging, but a registered dietitian can help with this process. Dietitians can help expand gluten-free food options, plan meals and ensure nutritional needs are being met. Despite its challenges, maintaining a healthy, balanced diet is possible with education and planning. The University of Tennessee Medical Center offers physician information, dietitian referral, and other reliable resources to help anyone follow a gluten-free lifestyle to treat celiac disease.

Refer to the online Celiac Center for more information about celiac disease by linking to the Healthy Living Kitchen's webpage. A gluten-free diet is not for everyone. The only reason someone should adopt a gluten-free diet is for the treatment of celiac disease or gluten intolerance. Gluten intolerance is a condition less severe than celiac disease where the body reacts to the presence of gluten. Sensitivity to gluten is now being recognized by the medical community thanks to recent medical research.

Celebrities have promoted gluten-free diets for "cleansing" or health, but this is not a good idea. Many gluten-free packaged items have more carbohydrates and less fiber. Eating gluten-free can cause vitamin and mineral deficiencies since fortified grain products are avoided. For the general public, it is best to eat a diet rich in fruits, vegetables, lean meats, dairy products, and whole-grains. The Healthy Living Kitchen has presented gluten-free cooking classes with special guest Janet Prince, author of *My Gluten-Free Knoxville*. Together, we promote a positive message about eating delicious, good-for-you, gluten-free meals while living a healthy life. Healthy Living Kitchen recipes use fresh, unprocessed ingredients, thus nearly 60% of the recipes in this book are gluten-free. We have denoted the gluten-free recipes throughout the cookbook, and there is a gluten-free recipe index in the back. Always make sure ingredients, such as soy sauce, are the gluten-free versions. Many recipes with a gluten-containing ingredient can be easily changed by substituting the gluten-free alternative.

Weight Management

When overweight, losing weight can improve heart disease risk by improving cholesterol, blood pressure, and blood glucose levels. Weight management is not easy, but getting started by setting achievable goals can help with motivation. Set your initial weight loss goal at 5–10% of your current weight. This amount alone has been shown to improve risk factors for certain diseases.

Calories Count

Calories are fuel for the body. Calories from food are either used as energy for the body or stored for later as body fat. Consuming too many calories and not burning enough through activity contributes to weight gain. Weight loss is achieved by eating fewer calories (or burning calories with exercise). To lose 1–2 pounds per week, decrease calorie intake by 500–1000 calories per day. This amount can be from eating less and/or increasing activity level. Calorie needs for each person vary based on gender, age, body size, and activity level. The lowest intake per day recommended for women is 1200 calories and for men is 1500 calories. If you are eating too few calories it can halt the weight loss process and may not meet your nutritional needs. Discuss your calorie needs with your doctor or registered dietitian.

Limit Liquid Calories

Every 8 ounces of soda, juice, sweet tea, lemonade, and milk equals 100 calories or more. Water is the best choice for staying hydrated. You can add a splash of 100% fruit juice for flavor.

Diet Foods

Many foods are marketed as sugar-free, fat-free or promoted for weight loss. If that food does not have fewer calories than the real thing it may not be a better choice. A good example is sugar-free cookies. Often these have even more calories per serving than regular cookies. Sometimes it is best to enjoy the real food but use portion control to keep calories controlled.

Control Appetite

Eat breakfast every day and avoid skipping meals. This helps keep your body from getting too hungry and helps control appetite. Strive for optimal nutrition by choosing foods that are high in fiber (fruits, vegetables, and whole grains) combined with lean proteins and healthy fats (chicken breast, yogurt, nuts, avocado). When planning meals and snacks combine high fiber foods with a protein or fat source, this works well to keep you satisfied for longer periods of time.

Mindful Eating

Listen to your body and take the time to enjoy food. Stop eating when you are getting full. Do not eat while standing or doing another task like watching TV.

Portion Control Matters

Use measuring cups when serving meals. Look at calories on the label as a way to guide choices. Eating from a smaller plate helps you feel more satisfied with normal portion sizes. When eating a snack, leave the food container in the kitchen while taking your portion with you.

Keep a Food Journal

Writing down what and how much you eat can help identify areas for improvement and may bring awareness to current eating habits. Studies show people lose more weight when keeping a food journal in the first 2–3 months of making a lifestyle change.

Successful weight loss takes time and effort. Making small changes with food choices and activity level help you keep the pace for a lifetime of weight management. Don't deprive yourself by eliminating certain foods. There are no foods you can never eat again. Planning ahead and using moderation helps to fit those foods into your diet without going overboard.

Exercise

Physical activity or exercise is a key ingredient in maintaining a healthy lifestyle. It is important that you find an activity you can enjoy and continue it on a regular basis to improve your personal health. Benefits of a regular exercise program include:

- Reduces your risk of heart disease, high blood pressure, osteoporosis, diabetes, and obesity

- Keeps joints, tendons, and ligaments flexible so it's easier to move around

- Reduces some of the effects of aging

- Improves your mood and helps you feel better overall

- Helps relieve stress and anxiety

- Boosts your energy level

- Improves your sleep

- Helps you burn calories and control weight

Types of Exercise

A well-rounded exercise program should incorporate three components: aerobic training, strength training, and stretching. Aerobic exercise is any continuous, rhythmic activity that uses your large muscle groups. Aerobic exercise elevates your heart rate, forcing your heart and lungs to work harder than at normal resting conditions. Examples of aerobic exercise are walking, jogging, hiking, and gardening. The American Heart Association recommends adults perform at least 150 minutes of moderate intensity aerobic physical activity (2 hours and 30 minutes) each week to help decrease the risk of heart disease and stroke. The second component, strength training, is a form of exercise in which an individual exerts force against a resistance. The resistance is typically some sort of weight or weight systems (i.e. dumbbells, resistance bands, weight machines, or one's own body weight). Strength training improves muscular strength and endurance and strengthens bones to increase bone density. Strength exercises should be performed 2-3 days a week, allowing at least 48 hours rest between each strength session for the same muscle groups. The third component is stretching and this form of exercise helps increase flexibility and range of motion. It is also a good exercise to do at bedtime for relaxation. The American College of Sports Medicine recommends to incorporate stretching 2-3 days a week for at least 10 minutes in duration. Stretching exercises should be performed to where there is slight discomfort, but nothing further!

How do I get started?

Start by talking with your doctor. This is especially important if you have not been active, if you have any health problems, if you are pregnant, or elderly.

Start out slowly. Begin with a 10-minute period of light exercise or a brisk walk every day and gradually increase how hard you exercise and the amount of time.

Build exercise into your everyday activities

- Take the stairs instead of the elevator.
- Go for a walk during your coffee break or lunch.
- Walk all or part of the way to work.
- Do housework at a fast pace.
- Rake leaves or do other yard work.

How do I stick with it?

- Choose an activity you enjoy doing.
- Get a partner. Exercising with someone else can make it more fun.
- Vary your routine. You may be less likely to get bored or injured if you change your routine. Walk one day. Bicycle the next. Consider activities like dancing and racquet sports and even household chores.
- Choose a comfortable time of day. Don't work out too soon after eating or when it's too hot or cold outside. Wait until later in the day if you're too stiff in the morning.
- Don't get discouraged. It can take weeks or months before you notice some of the changes from exercise.
- Forget "no pain, no gain." While a little soreness is normal after you first start exercising, pain isn't. Stop if you hurt.
- Make exercise fun. Read, listen to music, or watch TV while riding a stationary bicycle, for example.
- Find fun things to do, like taking a walk through the zoo. Go dancing. Learn how to play tennis.

Measuring Your Heart Rate

The number of times you feel your heartbeat in a minute is your heart rate. Press your finger gently next to your Adam's apple. Count the number of beats you feel for 10 seconds. Multiply by 6 to get your heart rate.

What is my target heart rate during exercise?

The following chart shows the target heart rates for people of different ages. When beginning an exercise program, shoot for the lower target heart rate (60%). As your fitness improves, you can exercise harder to get your heart rate closer to the top number (85%).

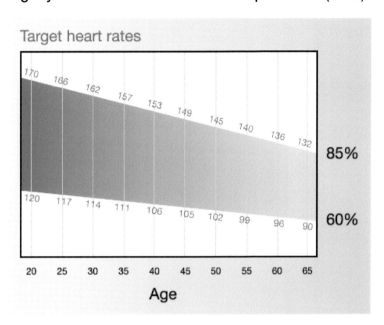

Other tools to help you in your exercise journey are exercise logs and pedometers. A pedometer helps you measure your daily steps and assists you in gradually increasing your daily activity. Record your steps on a daily activity log. Pedometers are also very beneficial for weight loss. These can be purchased at a sports store for a low cost.

Stress Management

Stress is a factor in everyone's life and if improperly managed can lead to many disease states. It can be as simple as noise in the room or complicated as a stressful relationship. Stress can be positive or negative in nature depending on how long it occurs and how it is perceived. Short-term stress can actually be beneficial in that it can make a person more alert, motivated, and productive. An example of short term stress is a work deadline. Unrelieved stress over a long period of time or chronic stress can have a negative effect on our bodies and minds. An example of chronic stress is receiving a diagnosis of cancer after taking care of a sick family member for an extended period of time.

A person's stress level is also dependent on their ability to cope with difficulties and challenges. What may be a stressful situation for one person may not be stressful for another. Individuals differ in the way they handle stress and possess different coping strategies. For example, one individual may consume alcohol and internalize their stress while another may choose to ventilate their feelings or exercise to release stress.

Disease, illness, employment status, work and home-life demands, support systems, coping skills, and finances impact an individual's ability to handle stress. It is important to recognize stress and its symptoms to prevent potential health problems.

Reaction to Stress

When your body perceives a threat or undergoes stress, signals are sent throughout your body to release hormones so that your body will have fuel to react to the threat. This has been labeled the "fight or flight" response. Once the threat is gone, your body should return to its normal state but sometimes this response continues due to the ongoing stress of daily life. Physical changes of this response are an increase in heart rate, breathing, and blood pressure. Stress causes arteries to constrict, blood to thicken, fat and sugar release for energy, digestion slows down, sweating increases, and the immune system slows down.

Symptoms of Stress

Stress brings about various symptoms. Some symptoms are very apparent while others can be subdued and attributed to other conditions. Many people seek medical attention for fatigue or back pain which can be caused by stress. That is why it is important to recognize stress and take measures to reduce it. Some of the symptoms of stress are:

- Anxiety, tension, depression, lack of concentration, irritability
- Abnormal eating patterns, increased tobacco or alcohol use, social withdrawal
- Difficulty sleeping, tiredness, sexual difficulty
- Aches, pains, fatigue
- Heartburn, indigestion, headaches

- Rapid heart rate, high blood pressure

Chronic stress can cause physical illness and disease. Some of the conditions or diseases that are attributed to stress are: heart disease, cancer, hypertension, stroke, depression, allergies, asthma, ulcers, migraine headaches, colitis, arthritis, and gout.

Your personal wellness depends on how you perceive stress and react to it. Understanding what triggers your stress response and identifying your stress symptoms will assist in managing your stress. It is also important to learn different techniques to decrease your stress level. Learning healthy ways to manage stress is vital in preventing stress-related conditions and diseases.

Managing Stress

Stress management is the key to healthier living. There are many coping methods that can help reduce stress in your life.

- Exercise and be physically active
- Eat a well-balanced diet full of fruits and vegetables
- Get plenty of sleep, 7–8 hours per night
- Give yourself permission to take time for yourself
- Be organized and prepare for everyday tasks
- Don't hold on to anger
- Minimize interruptions
- Know your limits and set boundaries
- Learn to say "no"
- Set realistic goals and expectations
- Learn good communication skills
- Practice positive thoughts
- Find humor in life
- Live, laugh, and love

Relaxation Techniques

It is impossible to alleviate stress completely. If we learn to manage stress and increase our ability to cope with everyday challenges, we can reduce our physical and mental responses to stressful situations. By practicing relaxation exercises, you will be able help your body produce the relaxation response, which helps slow your breathing, heart rate, and blood pressure, as well as relax your muscles and, ultimately, reduce the effects of stress hormones in your body. This will aid your body in fighting off diseases and relieve pain while increasing energy and focus. These exercises will allow you to feel more relaxed, a sense of calmness and peace, and view life in a more positive way. Stress management exercises that help with relaxation are:

- Meditation involves the practice of achieving thoughtless awareness in which the mind is free from stress by the use of quiet contemplation and reflection.

- Guided imagery focuses on the imagination to achieve a state of relaxation.

- Yoga is a series of stretches, poses, and breathing techniques that creates balance, strength, flexibility, and relaxation.

- Tai Chi is an ancient Chinese martial art, also called "meditation in motion" because it promotes serenity through gentle movements.

- Progressive muscle relaxation uses techniques to relieve tension by alternating tensing and relaxing the muscles.

By using these simple techniques, you can learn how to stay calm and maintain a sense of control. It's important you find what relaxation techniques works best for you and fits into your lifestyle. You can explore different techniques by using videos, taking classes, or reading books. Remember, relaxation doesn't happen immediately; it takes practice.

Culinary Skills

A basic understanding of culinary fundamentals makes it easier to cook fresh meals at home. In the Healthy Living Kitchen cooking classes, we demonstrate how to handle, chop, cut, and cook the ingredients for the recipes in order to increase the appearance and taste of your dishes. From how to dice an onion to proper sautéing techniques, we cover all the skills needed to be a solid cook. This book offers a mix of very easy recipes for the beginning cook to some recipes that are a bit more advanced. All recipes are tailored for the home cook to easily prepare. It is important to remember that recipes are just guidelines. Anyone can substitute items for their favorites as long as it is an even swap from a nutritional aspect. The following provides knife skills, recipe modifications and sample menus designed to improve your culinary skills.

Knife Skills

Basic knife skills are essential for any cook, whether you plan to earn a living in the kitchen or simply please yourself, your friends, and your family. Learning to use a knife correctly will speed up your prep time, and food products fashioned in uniform shapes and sizes will help guarantee even cooking throughout a dish. In addition, the mastery of certain classic knife cuts and methodology will greatly improve the look of your food, garnishes, and plate presentations.

The safe use of knives is imperative for obvious reasons. There are only a few rules to remember, but they are crucial:

- A sharp knife is a safe knife.
- Never grab a falling knife.
- Use the right knife for the right job.
- Always cut away from, never towards yourself.
- When you have a knife in hand, keep your eyes on the blade.
- Carry a knife properly.
- Never put a knife in a sink full of water.

Types of Knives

- **Chef's knife:** These knives are usually the largest knives in the kitchen, with a wide blade that is 8–10" in length. Choose a knife that feels good and balanced in your hand. The knife should have a full tang. This means the blade should go all the way through the handle for better wear and increased stability.

- **Paring knife:** These knives are generally 2½–4" in length. These are the most often used knives in the kitchen. It is ideal for peeling and coring fruits and vegetables, cutting small objects, slicing, and other hand tasks.

- **Utility knife:** These knives are longer than paring knives but smaller than chef's knives, usually around 5–8" in length. They are also called sandwich knives because they are just the right size for slicing meats and cheeses.

- **Boning knife:** This type of knife has a more flexible blade to curve around meat and bone. Generally 4–5" in length.

- **Bread knife:** These knives are usually serrated. Most experts recommend a serrated knife that has pointed serrations instead of wavy serrations for better control and longer knife life. It is suggested to have at least two bread knives in your kitchen: a long 10"-knife that's great for cutting whole loaves, and a 6"-knife perfect for cutting sandwich buns. Use a sawing motion when using a serrated knife.

Knife Sharpening Tips

- A sharp knife is safer than a dull one. Dull knives cause people to put more effort into cutting, and may also encourage unsafe cutting positions, both of which increase your chance of injury.

- Sharpen your knife with a wet sharpening stone, keeping an even 20°-angle throughout the swing (for a chef's knife). After sharpening a knife, wipe the blade off to remove any metal particles. All knives dull with use.

- Use a wood, bamboo, or synthetic, non-porous cutting board. Avoid marble or glass cutting boards as they will damage your knives.

- Do not bang the blade against pots, bowls, counters, or anything else as an effort to remove remaining food items.

- Do not cut string, paper, and tin cans with your knife.

- It is not a good idea to put knives in the dishwasher. The dishwasher dulls the blades and handles are not designed for the temperatures of a dishwasher.

- Always cut on a cutting board. Don't cut on metal, glass or marble. This will ultimately damage a knife's edge.

Types of Cuts

Chopping: Coarse chopping is generally used for mirepoix, a mixture of onions, carrots and celery or similar flavoring ingredients that are to be strained out of the dish and discarded. It is also used when cutting vegetables that are to be pureed. This is not a perfectly neat cut, but pieces need to be roughly the same size.

Mincing: Mincing is a fine cut that is good for many vegetables and herbs (onions, garlic, and shallots). For herbs:

- Rinse and dry herbs well. Strip the leaves from the stems. Gather the leaves in a pile on your cutting board.

- Using your guiding hand to hold them in place, position the knife so it can slice through the pile.
- Coarsely chop.
- Once the herbs are coarsely chopped, use the fingertips of your guiding hand to hold the tip of the knife to the cutting board. Keeping the tip of the blade on the cutting board, lower the knife firmly and rapidly cut through the herbs.

Classic Cuts: The following lists types and sizes of classic cuts.

- Julienne: 1/8 x 1–2"
- Fine julienne: 1/16 x 1–2"
- Large dice: 3/4 x 3/4"
- Medium dice: 1/2 x 1/2"
- Small dice: 1/4 x 1/4"
- Brunoise: 1/8 x 1/8"
- Fine brunoise: 1/16 x 1/16"

Chiffonade: Chiffonade is a fine slice or shred of leafy vegetables or herbs. To chiffonade, simply stack a few leaves, roll them into a cigar shape, and slice. Remember to remove any tough, woody stems that you want to exclude from your preparation.

Simple Substitutions for a Healthier Recipe

For Additional Fiber…

Instead of:	Try using:
White Flour	Whole Wheat Flour
White Rice	Brown Rice, Barley, Quinoa, Whole Wheat Couscous
Pastas, Crackers, Cereal	Whole Grain Pasta, Crackers, & Cereals
White Bread	100% Whole Wheat Bread and 100% Whole Grain Bread

Tips: Sneak extra fruit and veggies into recipes, and include the peel for extra fiber (ex: add carrots to spaghetti sauce or unpeeled apples to apple crisp). For added fiber in your baked goods add ground flax seed or oats.

To Lighten Up on Fats & Oils…

Instead of:	Try using:
Mayonnaise	Light Mayonnaise or Plain Non-Fat Yogurt
Sour Cream	Light Sour Cream or Non-Fat Greek Yogurt
Butter	Trans Free Margarine or Whipped Butter
Oil	Try using applesauce or prune puree to replace half the oil called for in a recipe

Tip: The fat in most recipes can be reduced by 1/3 without affecting the taste.

To Cut the Sugar…

Instead of:	Try using:
Sugar	• Splenda ® or Stevia baking blend. • Agave nectar - use 1/3 less than recipe calls for (if recipe calls for 1 cup sugar use 2/3 cup agave nectar), and lower the baking temperature by 25 degrees.

Tips: The sugar in most recipes can be reduced by 1/3 without affecting the taste. Cinnamon and vanilla or almond extract can be added to give the impression of sweetness.

To Reduce the Sodium…

Instead of:	Try using:
Salt	Omit salt or reduce by 1/2 , Kosher or Sea Salt may have less sodium depending on brand
Seasoning Salt	• Use salt-free seasonings like Mrs. Dash, garlic powder, onion powder, or pepper • Try using fresh or dried herbs

Tips: Do not put a salt shaker on the table. Rinse canned beans & vegetables to reduce their sodium content.

For the Skinny on Dairy…

Instead of:	Try using:
Whole Milk	Skim or 1% Milk
Cream	Evaporated Non-Fat Milk
Whole-Fat Cheese	Reduced Fat Cheese
Buttermilk	1 Tbsp vinegar or lemon juice, add skim milk to make 1 cup. Let stand for 5 minutes.

Helpful Kitchen Basics

Measurement Equivalents

3 teaspoons	1 tablespoon
4 tablespoons	¼ cup
2 tablespoons	1 ounce
¼ cup	2 ounces
½ cup	4 ounces
¾ cup	6 ounces
1 cup	8 ounces

Food Storage Times for the Freezer

Food	Freezer
Beef	6–12 months
Ground Beef	3–4 months
Pork	4–6 months
Chicken and Turkey	9–12 months
Fatty Fish	4 months
Lean Fish	8 months
Cooked Meat Dishes and Soups	2–3 months

Safe Minimum Internal Temperature

Food	Temperature (°F)	Rest Time
Ground Beef	160	None
Ground Turkey	165	None
Fresh Beef	145	3 minutes
Poultry	165	None
Fresh Pork	145	3 minutes
Casseroles and Leftovers	165	None

Sample Menus

Here are just a few examples of how the recipes in this book fit together for delicious, fresh, and good-for-you meals.

Valentine's Day

Spicy Shrimp and Asparagus Salad
Chicken Mediterranean Pasta
Chocolate Walnut Mousse Phyllo Cups with Fresh Fruit

Holiday Meal

Apple-Raisin Stuffed Pork Loin
Sautéed Asparagus with Roasted Red Peppers
Sweet Potato Crunch
Light Pumpkin Pudding

Farmer's Market

Garlic Herb Chicken Skewers
Golden Sun Potatoes
Swiss Chard and Onions
Grilled Peaches with Cinnamon, Walnuts, and Basil

Sample Menus

Family Meal

Oven Fried Garlic Chicken
Sweet Potato Salad
Summer Squash and Cherry Tomatoes
Broccoli Layer Salad
Strawberry Parfaits

Tailgating

Barbecue Chicken Wrap
Chipotle Portobello Sandwich
Black Bean Salsa with Baked Tortilla Chips
Crunchy Kickoff Coleslaw
Dark Chocolate Brownies
Pumpkin Spice Cupcakes

Holiday Appetizers

Herb Crusted Salmon
Turkey and Fig Skewers
Goat Cheese and Toasted Walnut Rounds
Pomegranate Fruit Salad
Fall Butternut Squash Quinoa
Maple Cream Cheese and Pecan Squares
Pumpkin Mousse Tarts

Recipes

First Courses

Featured: Spicy Shrimp and Asparagus Salad

Acorn Squash Soup

3 acorn squash

1 1/2 cups carrots, peeled and diced

1/2 cup celery, diced

1 cup onion, finely diced

4 cups vegetable broth

1/4 cup dry or cooking sherry

1/2 teaspoon salt

1/2 teaspoon black pepper

1 teaspoon garlic powder

1/4 teaspoon paprika

1/2 teaspoon nutmeg

1 cup fat-free half and half

1 pinch paprika for garnish (optional)

Cut squash in half, remove seeds. Place open side down and bake at 350F degrees in oven until soft, (approximately 55 minutes). Place cooked squash halves on paper towels on a baking pan and allow to cool. Scoop out the pulp and reserve. If desired, save the shells and cut the bottom so they can sit flat and use them as soup bowls. Sauté the carrots, celery, and onion until tender. Combine 1/2 of carrot mixture, 1/2 squash pulp, and 1 cup vegetable broth in an electric blender, cover and process until smooth. Place puree in a large saucepan. Repeat this procedure with the remaining carrot mixture, squash pulp, and vegetable broth. Add remaining vegetable broth, sherry, salt, garlic powder, pepper, paprika, and nutmeg. Simmer for 1 hour. Add half and half, stir, and serve in reserved acorn squash. Garnish with paprika.

Serving size: 1 cup

Yields: 8 cups

Nutrition Facts (per serving): 99 calories, 0g total fat, 0g saturated fat, 316mg sodium, 24.5g carbohydrates, 4g fiber, *Gluten-Free*

Healthy Living Tip

One serving (1/2 cup) of cooked acorn squash provides 20% (5 g) of daily recommended fiber and 10% (448 mg) of daily recommended potassium.

Baked Tortilla Chips

8 six-inch flour or corn tortillas

non-stick cooking spray

salt to taste

black pepper to taste

Preheat the oven to 350F degrees. Cut each tortilla into wedges and arrange the wedges in a single layer on non-stick baking sheets. Lightly spray the chips with oil and sprinkle with salt and pepper. Bake the chips for 10 to 15 minutes or until they are lightly browned and crisp turning with a spatula. Transfer the chips to a cake rack to cool.

Serving size: 1 tortilla cut into chips

Yields: 8 tortillas cut into chips

Nutrition Facts (per serving): 100 calories, 2g total fat, 0g saturated fat, 150mg sodium, 12g carbohydrates, 0g fiber.

Healthy Living Tip

Try whole wheat, spinach, or sun-dried tomato tortillas. Add a dash of cayenne pepper for spicier chips.

Beef Tenderloin Canapés with Mustard-Horseradish Sauce

2/3 cup fat-free sour cream

1/4 cup Dijon mustard

2 tablespoons minced fresh tarragon

2 tablespoons prepared horseradish

1 1/2 pounds beef tenderloin, trimmed

1/2 teaspoon freshly ground black pepper

non-stick cooking spray

2 tablespoons fresh lemon juice

3 cups baby arugula

8 ounces French bread multigrain baguette, cut diagonally into 16 pieces

2 ounces Parmesan cheese, fresh, shaved

Preheat oven to 350F degrees. Combine the sour cream, mustard, tarragon and horseradish, stirring well with a whisk, then cover and chill. Season the beef with pepper. Heat a large non-stick skillet over medium-high heat and coat the pan with cooking spray. Sear the beef on both sides and finish in the oven to the desired doneness. For medium, roast for 20 minutes or until the internal temperature reaches 133F–139F degrees and has a hot red, pink center. Let stand for 10 minutes. Cut into 16 slices, and sprinkle with lemon juice. Place arugula evenly on bread slices and place 1 beef slice and about 1 tablespoon of chilled sauce over each bread slice. Top with cheese.

Serving size: 1 canapé

Yields: 16 servings

Nutrition Facts (per serving): 128 calories, 5g total fat, 1.8g saturated fat, 275mg sodium, 10g carbohydrates, 1g fiber.

Healthy Living Tip

Arugula is a leafy green vegetable that has a slightly bitter flavor. Arugula is often used as a salad green and can also be cooked in pastas for an addition of calcium, folate, and vitamins A and C.

Black Bean Salsa

1 15-ounce can black beans, drained, rinsed

1 11-ounce can corn, no-added-salt

1 15-ounce can dice tomatoes, no-added-salt

1/2 cup orange bell pepper, diced

1 jalapeno pepper, diced

1/4 cup red onion or green onion, diced

3 tablespoons chopped fresh cilantro

2 tablespoons red wine vinegar

juice from 1 fresh lime

1 teaspoon cumin

1 tablespoon olive oil

black pepper to taste

Mix all ingredients together and serve. This is a great recipe to make the night before.

Serving size: approximately 1/2 cup

Yields: 12 servings

Nutrition Facts (per serving): 80 calories, 1.5g total fat, 0g saturated fat, 71mg sodium, 13g carbohydrates, 3.5g fiber, *Gluten-Free*

Healthy Living Tip

Drain and rinse canned beans to reduce sodium content by 30%. Reduce sodium in canned vegetables by selecting no-added-salt varieties.

Caramelized Onion Dip

3 small red onions, chopped (2 ½ to 3 cups)

2 tablespoons olive oil

2 cloves garlic, minced

1/2 tablespoon chopped fresh ginger

1/2 teaspoon chopped fresh thyme leaves

1/2 teaspoon chopped fresh rosemary

salt and pepper to taste

1/2 teaspoon agave nectar

1 cup low-fat sour cream

Heat the oil in a large skillet. Stir in the chopped red onions, garlic, thyme leaves and rosemary; season with salt and pepper. Cook in the skillet, stirring for 10 minutes or until it is very soft and starting to brown. Stir in the agave nectar then let it cool. Stir in the sour cream, cover and allow to stand at least an hour before serving.

Serving size: 2 tablespoons

Yields: approximately 2 cups

Nutrition Facts (per serving): 49 calories, 4g total fat, 1g saturated fat, 10mg sodium, 4g carbohydrates, 0g fiber, *Gluten-Free*

Chicken Satay

1 pound chicken breast

1/2 cup Dijon mustard

1/3 cup honey

1/3 cup natural peanut butter

1 teaspoon garlic, chopped

1 teaspoon ginger, minced

2 tablespoons soy sauce, light

Soak wooden skewers in water overnight prior to using. Combine all ingredients except the chicken to make the sauce. Cut chicken in 1/4-inch strips and place on skewers. Marinate chicken in 1/4 of the sauce, reserving 3/4 of the sauce for dipping. Grill on medium-high heat to doneness and serve with dipping sauce.

Serving Size: 1 skewer and 1 tablespoon dipping sauce

Yields: 12 servings

Nutrition Facts (per serving): 86 calories, 4g total fat, 1g saturated fat, 211mg sodium, 10g carbohydrates, 1g fiber, *Gluten-Free*

Healthy Living Tip

When cooking chicken, use a meat thermometer to ensure an internal temperature of 160F. The breast meat is 30% lower in saturated fat content compared with its dark meat counterparts. To cut fat content in half, remove the skin from the chicken or simply buy skinless chicken breasts.

Chilled Shrimp with Low-sodium Cocktail Sauce and Walnut Pesto

Shrimp

1 tablespoon olive oil

2 tablespoons Mrs. Dash Extra Spicy Seasoning

2 tablespoons lemon juice

2 pounds 26/30 count shrimp, peeled and deveined

Low-sodium Cocktail Sauce

1/4 cup no-salt-added ketchup

2 tablespoons white wine vinegar

2 tablespoons fresh lemon juice

1 teaspoon agave nectar

1 tablespoon prepared white horseradish

Walnut Pesto

1 1/2 cups packed fresh flat-leaf parsley leaves

1 cup packed fresh basil

1 1/2 tablespoons walnut pieces

3 tablespoons cold water

2 tablespoons extra virgin olive oil

2 tablespoons red wine vinegar

2 teaspoons Dijon mustard

1/4 teaspoon salt

1/8 teaspoon freshly ground black pepper

1 garlic clove, peeled and smashed

To prepare the shrimp: combine all ingredients and cook over a preheated grill or in a sauté pan over medium-high heat for about 1-2 minutes on each side. Do not overcook. Chill for 1 hour.

To prepare the pesto: combine all 10 ingredients in a blender and process until smooth. Pour into a bowl, cover and chill.

To prepare the cocktail sauce: combine all the ingredients (add hot pepper sauce, if desired), cover and chill.

Serve the shrimp with the sauces.

Serving size: 5 shrimp and 1 tablespoon each sauce.

Yields: 12 servings.

Nutrition Facts (per serving): 82 calories, 5g total fat, 0g saturated fat, 112mg sodium, 3g carbohydrates, 0g fiber, *Gluten-Free*

Gazpacho

1 cup water

1 cup tomato puree

1/2 cup bulgur

2 tablespoons balsamic vinegar

1 clove garlic, minced

1/2 teaspoon cumin

1 teaspoon salt

1 1/4 teaspoons hot pepper sauce

4 scallions, sliced

1 cup tomatoes, roughly chopped

1 cup seeded cucumbers, peeled, seeded, diced

3/4 cup green bell pepper, diced

3 tablespoons fresh cilantro, chopped

black pepper to taste

Bring the water and 1/2 the tomato puree to a boil. Pour over the bulgur and cover for 20 minutes. Fluff with a fork. Combine remaining ingredients with bulgur and chill.

Serving size: 1 cup

Yields: 6 servings

Nutrition Facts (per serving): 100 calories, 0g total fat, 0g saturated fat, 400mg sodium, 23g carbohydrates, 5g fiber.

Healthy Living Tip

Gazpacho is a chilled, tomato-based soup. It is low in calories, rich in flavor, antioxidants, and fiber.

Goat Cheese and Toasted Walnut Rounds

1 ounce walnuts

1 teaspoon olive oil

1/8 teaspoon cinnamon

Kosher salt and black pepper

6 ounces soft goat cheese

1/2 cup dried cranberries

1/2 teaspoon fresh thyme, chopped

Preheat oven to 375F degrees. In a medium bowl, toss nuts with 1 teaspoon of olive oil. Mix in the cinnamon, salt and pepper. Spread the nut mixture on a baking sheet and bake about 5 minutes or until toasted then allow to cool. Finely chop the nuts and place in a shallow dish. In a medium bowl mix the goat cheese and thyme. Scoop a heaping 1/2 teaspoon of goat cheese mixture and press a few pieces of cranberries into the center, then wrap the cheese around the dried fruit to form a ball. Roll the ball in the chopped nuts to form a crust and set on a serving tray. Repeat with the remaining goat cheese, dried fruit and nuts.

Serving size: 2 pieces

Yields: 24 pieces

Nutrition Facts (per serving): 72 calories, 5g total fat, 2g saturated fat, 75mg sodium, 5g carbohydrates, 0g fiber.

Healthy Living Tip

Although it should be used in moderation, goat cheese provides approximately 20% daily recommended intake (DRI) of vitamin A and 22% DRI of phosphorous. Phosphorous is major contributor to bone and teeth health, second only to calcium.

Herb Crusted Salmon with Cucumber Dill Cream

16 ounces salmon fillet, skin off

1 tablespoon Dijon mustard

1 teaspoon dried Italian seasoning

¼ cup cucumber peeled, seeded and cut into 1/4-inch cubes

1 pinch Kosher salt

6 ounces fat-free sour cream

2 tablespoons dried dill weed

Mix together mustard and Italian herb blend. Top the salmon with the mustard blend and cut the fish into 2 ounce squares, then place on a sprayed sheet pan. Mix together the remaining ingredients in a separate bowl and store in the refrigerator. Roast the salmon in a 350F degree oven for 8-12 minutes or until the salmon has an internal temperature of 160F degrees. Top with dill sauce.

Serving size: 2- 2 ounce squares

Yields: 8 servings

Nutrition Facts (per serving): 123 calories, 6g total fat, 1g saturated fat, 113mg sodium, 6g carbohydrates, 0g fiber, *Gluten-Free*

Healthy Living Tip

The American Heart Association recommends eating fatty fish such as salmon at least twice a week for a boost of heart-healthy omega-3 fatty acids.

Holiday Turkey Meatballs

Meatballs

1 pound ground turkey, 93% lean

2/3 cup grated carrots

1 large Omega-3 egg

1/2 cup old-fashioned oats

1/2 cup grated Parmesan cheese

2 tablespoons ground flaxseed

1 tablespoon garlic powder

1/2 teaspoon Kosher salt

1/8 teaspoon pepper

non-stick cooking spray

Cranberry Sauce

1 bag fresh cranberries

1/3 cup agave nectar

1 cup orange juice

1 12-ounce bottle chili sauce

Preheat the oven to 400F degrees. Spray a large baking sheet with non-stick cooking spray and set aside. Combine the turkey, carrots, egg, oats, Parmesan cheese, flaxseed, and spices in a large bowl and mix until ingredients are just combined. Shape the meat mixture into 48 cocktail size balls. Place them on the baking sheet and cook them for 10-12 minutes or until they are lightly browned. Combine the cranberries, agave, and orange juice in a large saucepan and cook over medium heat, whisking occasionally, until the cranberry mixture is reduced by half, then add the chili sauce. When the meatballs come out of the oven, add them to the sauce, then reduce the heat and simmer, covered, for about 20 minutes.

Serving size: 4 mini-meatballs

Yields: 12 servings

Nutrition Facts (per serving): 135 calories, 5g total fat, 1.5g saturated fat, 200mg sodium, 9g carbohydrates, 1g fiber.

Healthy Living Tip

The meatball recipe makes a great entree by preparing larger size meatballs and adding a low-sodium marinara sauce.

Low Fat Corn Bread Stuffing Cakes

Cornbread

1 1/4 cup yellow corn meal (stone-ground preferred)

1 cup all-purpose flour

1 tablespoon baking powder

2 tablespoons sugar

3/4 cup fat-free (skim) milk

3 large egg whites

2 tablespoons melted butter or trans-free margarine

1 (10-ounce size) package frozen corn, thawed and drained

Stuffing

2 cups onion, diced

1 cup celery, diced

1 cup red bell pepper, diced

2 cups reduced-fat/sodium chicken broth, divided

1 large bunch Swiss chard, chopped

1 egg white

1 teaspoon fennel seeds

1/4 teaspoon salt

1/2 teaspoon freshly ground black pepper

1/4 teaspoon red pepper flakes

non-stick pan spray for pans

Corn Bread: Heat oven to 400F degrees. Spray an 8-inch baking pan. Combine cornmeal, flour, sugar, and baking powder in bowl. Stir in milk, egg whites, melted butter and corn. Pour into the prepared pan. Bake 25 minutes or until a toothpick inserted in the center comes out clean. Cool and crumble. Spray one or two mini muffin baking pans, then set aside.

Stuffing: Combine onions, celery, diced bell pepper and 1/2 cup of the chicken broth in a sauce pan. Cook over medium heat 10 minutes, stirring frequently. Add chopped Swiss chard; cover and cook 2 minutes. Remove from heat. Stir in crumbled corn bread, egg white, the remaining 1 1/2 cups chicken broth, fennel seed, salt, black pepper and red pepper flakes. Spoon stuffing mixture into muffin pan; cover and bake 20-30 minutes. Uncover and bake 10 minutes more.

Serving size: 1 stuffing cake

Yields: 20 cakes

Nutrition Facts (per serving): 128 calories, 1g total fat, 0g saturated fat, 189mg sodium, 21g carbohydrates, 3.5g fiber.

Healthy Living Tip

To assemble Roasted Turkey Breast on "Stuffing" Cake with Cranberry Apple Relish:

Start with stuffing cake, top with turkey breast then dollop cranberry relish.

Pico de Gallo

2 large tomatoes, diced

1 small onion, chopped

2 tablespoons fresh cilantro chopped

juice from 1 fresh lime

1/2 green pepper, diced

1 jalapeno pepper, diced

salt and pepper to taste

Mix and serve with baked tortilla chips.

Serving size: 1/2 cup

Yields: approximately 2 cups

Nutrition Facts (per serving): 30 calories, <1g total fat, <1g saturated fat, 70mg sodium, 6g carbohydrates, 2g fiber, *Gluten-Free*

Healthy Living Tip

When storing fresh herbs, place them in a glass of water and cover with a plastic bag. To increase freshness, trim the ends of the herbs. To check freshness, rub the herb between your fingers and check the strength of its aroma.

Pomegranate Fruit Salad

Dressing

1/2 cup pomegranate juice

4 tablespoons honey

4 tablespoons olive oil

2 tablespoons red wine vinegar

2 tablespoons chopped mint

2 tablespoons plain yogurt

Salad

1 cup arils (seeds) from 1 pomegranate

2 pears, peeled and sliced

1 cup fresh pineapple chunks

1 can Mandarin oranges, no sugar added

1 tablespoon fresh mint sliced

3 cups mixed greens

salt and pepper to taste

Dressing: Combine ingredients in a medium bowl and whisk until incorporated. Set aside or refrigerate for up to 2 days before serving.

Salad: Split a fresh pomegranate in half lengthwise and submerge the two halves in a bowl of water. Break open the pomegranate under the water to free the arils (seeds). The arils will sink to the bottom of the bowl and the membrane will float to the top. Sieve and put the arils in a separate bowl. Reserve 1 cup of the arils from the fruit and set aside. In a large bowl, place the Mandarin oranges including the juice, then add the pear slices and pineapple chunks. Place a base of mixed greens on six plates and divide the fruit mix on top. Garnish with pomegranate seeds and serve with the dressing on the side.

Serving size: 1/6 recipe

Yields: 6 servings

Nutrition Facts (per serving): 140 calories, 5g total fat, <1g saturated fat, 60mg sodium, 24g carbohydrates, 2.5g fiber, *Gluten-Free*

Healthy Living Tip

Pomegranates are an excellent source of antioxidant vitamins A and C as well as folate and potassium. Pomegranate juice's antioxidant quality is greater than red wine, green tea, and blueberry juice.

Roasted Garlic Spread

4 whole heads garlic

4 tablespoons olive oil

dash sea salt

Lay each head of garlic on its side and cut off 1/2-inch across the top. Place each head in an individual ovenproof dish. Drizzle with olive oil and cover with foil, then bake at 350F degrees for 45-60 minutes, or until the garlic is tender when tested with a fork. Using a fork, make a spread by releasing the garlic from the skins right onto a baking dish and stir it into the oil. Sprinkle with coarse salt and serve with toasted wholegrain baguette slices.

Serving size: 1/4 recipe

Yields: 4 servings

Nutrition Facts (per serving): 124 calories, 14g total fat, 2g saturated fat, 65mg sodium, 1g carbohydrates, 0g fiber, *Gluten-Free*

Healthy Living Tip

Eating a clove of fresh garlic per day may lower cholesterol and blood pressure. Garlic supplements do not have the phytonutrients found in fresh garlic and are not likely to provide the same benefits.

Salmon Party Roll

1 15-ounce can red salmon

1 8-ounce 1/3 less fat cream cheese, softened

1 tablespoon lemon juice

2 teaspoons grated onion

1 tablespoon prepared horseradish

1 1/2 teaspoons dill

1/2 cup pecans, chopped

3 tablespoons fresh parsley, minced

2 tablespoons red bell pepper, diced

fresh rosemary

Drain the salmon then flake it with a fork. Add the cream cheese, lemon juice, onion, horseradish and dill, then stir it well. Chill the mixture for several hours or overnight. Shape the salmon mixture into a ring. Combine pecans, red pepper, and parsley, then stir well. Sprinkle pecan mixture on top of ring and pat the mixture into a ring. Chill for several hours, then garnish with fresh rosemary sprigs and red pepper.

Serving size: 1/12 recipe

Yields: 12 servings

Nutrition Facts (per serving): 125 calories, 8g total fat, 2.6g saturated fat, 200mg sodium, 2g carbohydrates, <1g fiber, **_Gluten-Free_**

Spicy Chicken Lettuce Wraps

1 tablespoon sesame oil

1 tablespoon minced garlic

1 pound boneless, skinless chicken breast, cut into 1/2-inch cubes

3 tablespoons hot pepper sauce

1 tablespoon sugar

1 tablespoon soy sauce

1 (8-ounce) can water chestnuts, drained and chopped

3 green onions, chopped

1/3 cup dry roasted peanuts, unsalted

1/2 head iceberg lettuce, separated into whole leaves

Heat the oil in a wok or large skillet over high heat, then add the garlic and cook for 30 seconds. Add chicken and cook for about 3 minutes or until the chicken is no longer pink inside, stirring frequently. Stir in the hot pepper and soy sauces, the sugar and stir-fry for 2 minutes. Add water chestnuts and cook for 3 more minutes. Finally, add green onions and cook for 2 minutes more. For each wrap, spoon a small amount of the mixture onto a lettuce leaf. Wrap the lettuce to enclose the filling. Serve immediately.

Serving size: 2 wraps

Yields: 12 servings

Nutrition Facts (per serving): 93 calories, 4g total fat, 1g saturated fat, 82mg sodium, 4g carbohydrates, 1g fiber, *Gluten-Free*

Healthy Living Tip

Make sure your soy sauce is a gluten-free brand, if following the gluten-free diet.

Spicy Mango Salsa

2 cups diced fresh mango

2 cups fresh peaches, pitted and chopped

2 cloves garlic, minced

2 tablespoons chopped fresh ginger root

1/4 cup chopped fresh basil

2 Serrano chili peppers, diced

1/4 cup fresh lime juice

In a large bowl, mix the mangoes, peaches, garlic, ginger and basil together. Add the chilies and lime juice to taste, then mix well. Allow to chill for 2 hours before serving.

Serving size: 1/2 cup

Yields: 8 servings

Nutrition Facts (per serving): 27 calories, 0g total fat, 0g saturated fat, 0mg sodium, 7g carbohydrates, 1g fiber, **_Gluten-Free_**

Spicy Shrimp and Asparagus Salad

Dressing

1 teaspoon Dijon mustard

1/3 cup fresh orange juice

1 teaspoon fresh lemon juice

1 tablespoon chopped fresh garlic

2/3 cup extra-virgin olive oil

1 tablespoon finely chopped fresh scallions (wash and dry before chopping)

Salad

1 pound thin asparagus, trimmed

1 pound medium shrimp (about 30), shelled and deveined

1 tablespoon olive oil

1/2 tablespoon chopped garlic

1 teaspoon crushed red pepper

1/2 teaspoon chopped parsley

salt and pepper to taste

3 cups spring mix rinsed and dried

1/2 tablespoon sliced red onion

4 1/2 cup cherry or grape tomatoes (halved)

1 tablespoon Parmesan cheese

Dressing: In a small bowl whisk the mustard, orange and lemon juices, scallions and garlic together. Add the oil in a stream, whisking until it is emulsified, then season with salt and pepper. Dressing may be prepared up to this point one day ahead and chilled but make sure to keep it covered. Bring the dressing to room temperature before proceeding and have a large bowl of ice water ready.

Salad: Cook the asparagus for about 3 1/2 minutes or until crisp-tender in a large saucepan of boiling salted water. Transfer the asparagus with a slotted spoon to the ice water to stop the cooking. Drain the asparagus in a colander and pat dry with paper towels. In a preheated sauté pan, add oil, chopped garlic, and crushed red pepper, then sauté briefly and add the shrimp and parsley cooking them for about 2 minutes, or until they are just about done. In a bowl toss in 1/3 cup of the dressing, the asparagus, shrimp, spring mix, tomatoes, and onions together, then salt and pepper to taste. Drizzle some of the remaining dressing on the salad and garnish with cheese.

Serving size: 1/6 recipe

Yields: 6 servings

Nutrition Facts (per serving): 180 calories, 11g total fat, 2g saturated fat, 121mg sodium, 12g carbohydrates, 4g fiber, *Gluten-Free*

Spinach Dip

3 cups plain, low-fat yogurt

1 envelope ranch dressing mix

1 10-ounce package frozen chopped spinach, thawed and well drained

1 8-ounce can water chestnuts, drained and chopped

1/4 cup red bell pepper, diced

1/2 cup artichokes, chopped

Line a strainer with cheesecloth and place it over a deep bowl. Add the yogurt to the strainer, cover and refrigerate overnight. The yogurt will drain and thicken overnight. Discard the liquid. This can be done in advance and stored for up to one week. Mix in the ranch seasoning with the prepared yogurt. Add the spinach, water chestnuts, red pepper, and artichokes and chill for at least 30 minutes before serving. Garnish with some extra red pepper slices and serve with fresh vegetables and pita wedges. This makes 2 cups of yogurt mixture.

Serving size: 2 tablespoons

Yields: 24 servings

Nutrition Facts (per serving): 23 calories, 0g total fat, 0g saturated fat, 173mg sodium, 3g carbohydrates, 1g fiber.

Stuffed Mushrooms

20 medium mushrooms

3 tablespoons trans-free margarine

2 tablespoons white onion, chopped

3 tablespoons red bell pepper, chopped

1/2 cup whole wheat crackers, crushed

2 tablespoons Parmesan cheese grated

1/2 teaspoon Italian blend seasoning

1 6-ounce can crab, drained and flaked (optional)

Preheat oven to 400F degrees. Remove the stems from the mushrooms and chop 1/4 cup of the stems. Cover and refrigerate the remaining stems for other use. Melt margarine in a large skillet on medium heat, then add a cup of chopped mushroom stems, onions, and peppers. Cook and stir until the vegetables are tender. Stir in cracker crumbs, cheese and Italian seasoning (and the crab meat, if desired). Spoon and crumb the mixture evenly into the mushroom caps, then place them on an ungreased baking sheet. Bake the mushroom caps for 15 minutes or until they are heated through.

Serving size: 2 mushrooms

Yields: 20 mushrooms

Nutrition Facts (per serving): 60 calories, 4g total fat, 1g saturated fat, 70mg sodium, 4g carbohydrates, 2g fiber.

Traditional Hummus

2 15-ounce cans garbanzo beans, rinsed and drained

2 garlic cloves, crushed

1/2 cup water

1/4 cup sesame seed paste (tahini)

3 tablespoons fresh lemon juice

2 tablespoons extra-virgin olive oil

3/4 teaspoon salt

1/4 teaspoon black pepper

Place beans and garlic in a food processor and pulse until chopped. Add 1/2 cup of water and the remaining ingredients, then pulse until smooth, scraping down the sides as needed.

Serving size: 2 tablespoons

Yields: 26 servings

Nutrition Facts (per serving): 44 calories, 2.5g total fat, 0g saturated fat, 74mg sodium, 4.4g carbohydrates, 1g fiber, *Gluten-Free*

Healthy Living Tip

Hummus is a healthy snack when paired with fresh vegetables and pita chips. Try hummus instead of mayonnaise on your next sandwich or wrap.

Traditional Tomato Bruschetta

2 cups tomatoes, diced

1 tablespoon garlic, minced

2 tablespoons fresh basil

1/4 cup Parmesan cheese, shredded

1/4 cup sun-dried tomatoes, diced

extra virgin olive oil

1 loaf baguette bread

In large bowl combine tomatoes, garlic, basil, Parmesan cheese, and sun-dried tomatoes. Slice the bread into 1/2-inch rounds, then toast the bread rounds in the oven on 350F degrees until golden brown (6–8 minutes). Remove the bread rounds from the oven, then top with tomato mixture and return to the oven to heat through. Serve immediately.

Serving size: 1 prepared round

Yields: 1 loaf baguette bread

Nutrition Facts (per serving): 75 calories, 3.5g total fat, 0g saturated fat, 70mg sodium, 8g carbohydrates, 1g fiber.

Tri Color Tomato Salad

1 red tomato

1 yellow tomato

1 green tomato

non-stick spray

salt to taste

pepper to taste

4 ounces sheep milk cheese

8 teaspoons olive oil

2 tablespoons balsamic vinegar

2 tablespoons fresh oregano, chopped

1 tablespoon fresh basil, chiffonade

Cut all the tomatoes in 8 wedges. Roast the green tomatoes on a sheet pan at 450F degrees for approximately 20 minutes or until caramelized on the outside and softened. Arrange a red, yellow and green tomato on a plate. Cut the cheese into thin slices and arrange 1 slice of cheese between each piece of tomato. Drizzle with olive oil and balsamic vinegar. Sprinkle with oregano and basil.

Serving size: 1/8 recipe

Yields: 8 servings

Nutrition Facts (per serving): 87 calories, 7g total fat, 2g saturated fat, 177mg sodium, 3g carbohydrates, 1g fiber, *Gluten-Free*

Healthy Living Tip

Roasted green tomatoes are a tasty lower calorie alternative to fried green tomatoes.

Turkey and Fig Skewers

8 ounces turkey breast, cubed

1 tablespoon fresh rosemary, chopped

1 pinch black pepper freshly ground

1 tablespoon extra virgin olive oil

8 dried figs, cut in half

1 tablespoon sherry

2 ounces orange juice

8 wooden skewers, pre-soaked

Place figs, sherry and orange juice in a small sauce pan and bring to a simmer and allow mixture to re-hydrate. Remove from heat and let it cool before proceeding. Toss the diced turkey breast with rosemary, olive oil and pepper, then skewer two pieces of turkey and two fig halves, starting with a fig and alternating. Grill the turkey for approximately 5-6 minutes on each side or until browned or done.

Serving size: 2 skewers

Yields: 8 skewers

Nutrition Facts (per serving): 141 calories, 4g total fat, 1g saturated fat, 54mg sodium, 12g carbohydrates, 2g fiber, *Gluten-Free*

Main Courses

Featured: Grilled Halibut with Corn Sauté and Quinoa Stir-Fry with Chicken

Apple Raisin Stuffed Pork Loin

3 pounds pork loin, natural or organic for less sodium

2 Fuji apples, cored, peeled and diced

1/4 cup golden raisins

1/4 cup Splenda

1/2 teaspoon salt

1/2 teaspoon black pepper

1/4 teaspoon cloves, ground

1/4 teaspoon cinnamon, ground

1/2 tablespoon canola oil

Stuffing: In a large bowl, add water with a splash of lemon juice to keep the apples from turning brown. Quarter, seed, and chop apples into 1/4-inch cubes and put them in the water for 1 minute, then drain. Place sauté pan over medium heat and add oil. When the oil is hot, place the remaining ingredients in a pan and sauté for 4 minutes or until heated through and raisins are soft stirring. You may need to constantly stir to keep the sugar from burning on the bottom of the pan. Set aside and let cool.

Roast: Butterfly the roast by first cutting lengthwise about halfway through the roast, then angle the knife and cut horizontally almost all of the way through on both sides. Unfold the pork and cut tiny slits in the surface of the meat. Cover with 2 layers of plastic wrap, then pound the loin with a meat mallet to flatten it as much as possible. Remove the plastic wrap and spread the mixture over the surface of the pork. Starting with the smallest side of the meat (which should be in the shape of a rectangle), roll it up tightly and secure it with kitchen string. Bake the pork loin at 325F degrees for 70 minutes or until the internal temperature reaches 155F degrees. Pull it from the oven and let it rest for about 10 minutes. Remove the strings and cut in 1/2-inch slices with a sharp knife.

Serving size: 4 ounces

Yields: 9 servings

Nutrition Facts (per serving): 180 calories, 7g total fat, 3g saturated fat, 55mg sodium, 11g carbohydrates, 1g fiber, *Gluten-Free*

Baked Whole Wheat Spaghetti

12 ounces uncooked whole wheat spaghetti

1 tablespoon extra virgin olive oil

1 small green pepper, diced

1 small red pepper, diced

1 small onion, diced

3 cloves garlic, chopped

1 bay leaf

1/2 teaspoon dried oregano

1/2 teaspoon dried basil

1/2 teaspoon dried thyme

1/2 cup Burgundy wine or red wine

2 jars tomato sauce, no-salt-added

1/4 cup shredded Parmesan cheese

3/4 cup shredded mozzarella cheese

Add olive oil to a pan and heat on medium-high until hot. Add the onions, garlic and herbs, then cook for 3-5 minutes until the onions begin to turn translucent. Now, add the peppers and continue to cook for 3-5 minutes or until the peppers become soft. Next, add the wine and cook for 3-5 minutes until the wine is almost evaporated. Add the tomato sauce and simmer for 20 minutes. While the sauce is simmering, boil the pasta until it is just done (al dente). Add the pasta to the mixture and mix well. Place the pasta and sauce in a sprayed 9 x 13 pan, then top with cheese and bake at 350F degrees for 20-25 minutes or until bubbly and golden.

Serving size: 1/9 recipe

Yields: 9 servings

Nutrition Facts (per serving): 250 calories, 4g total fat, 2g saturated fat, 275mg sodium, 33g carbohydrates, 2g fiber.

Healthy Living Tip

When selecting a base tomato sauce, check the food label. Choose a jar that has less than 350 mg sodium per serving.

Catfish Parmesan

1/2 cup grated, reduced-fat Parmesan cheese

1/4 cup Panko bread crumbs

1/2 teaspoon black pepper

1 teaspoon paprika

1/2 teaspoon Italian blend seasoning

2 pounds catfish fillets, skinless

2-3 egg whites

2 tablespoons trans-free margarine

non-stick cooking spray

In a medium sized bowl, combine the Parmesan cheese, flour and seasonings. In a separate bowl, beat the egg whites. Dip the catfish in egg whites, then coat with the cheese mixture. Place fish in a baking dish sprayed with cooking spray and pour margarine over the catfish and bake for approximately 15-20 minutes at 400F degrees until golden brown and the fish flakes when tested with a fork.

Serving size: 4 ounces

Yields: 6 servings

Nutrition Facts (per serving): 227 calories, 8g total fat, 2.5g saturated fat, 269mg sodium, 8g carbohydrates, 2g fiber.

Healthy Living Tip

Panko bread crumbs originate in Japan. They have a flaky, airy texture and absorb less oil.

Chicken Jambalaya

1 teaspoon extra virgin olive oil

4 ounces low-fat smoked sausage

1 medium yellow onion, chopped

2 stalks celery, finely chopped

12 ounces boneless, skinless chicken breast, cut into 1-inch pieces

1/2 medium red bell pepper, chopped

1/2 medium green bell pepper, chopped

3/4 cup uncooked long grain rice

3 medium garlic cloves, minced

1 teaspoon salt-free Cajun seasoning or extra spicy salt free seasoning

1/2 teaspoon dried thyme, crumbled

1/2 teaspoon dried oregano, crumbled

1 14.5-ounce can no-added-salt diced tomatoes with juice

3/4 cup fat-free, low-sodium chicken broth

hot pepper sauce

Add oil to a large sauce pot and heat over medium heat. Add the chicken and cook 2-3 minutes. Add the sausage and cook for 2-3 minutes. Stir in the peppers, onion, and celery and cook for another 4-5 minutes, stirring frequently. Reduce the heat to medium low. Add the rice, garlic, seasoning blend, thyme, and oregano and cook for 2 minutes stirring frequently. Finally, stir in the tomatoes and broth and increase the heat to a boil. Reduce heat and simmer, covered for 20 minutes, or until the rice is thoroughly cooked.

Serving size: 1 1/2 cups

Yields: 4 servings

Nutrition Facts (per serving): 302 calories, 4g total fat, 1g saturated fat, 378mg sodium, 38g carbohydrates, 3g fiber.

Healthy Living Tip

Any recipe can be modified to fit into a heart healthy eating plan. The small amount of smoked sausage, salt-free Cajun seasoning, and reduced sodium chicken broth, make this a healthier version of jambalaya.

Chicken Mediterranean Pasta

Pasta

2 tablespoons extra virgin olive oil

½ cup crimini mushrooms

1/2 teaspoon chopped garlic

4 ounces sliced grilled herb marinated chicken

1 tablespoon sun-dried tomatoes

1 tablespoon fresh basil

½ cup low-sodium chicken stock

1 tablespoon cornstarch

1 tablespoon feta cheese

1 pinch salt and freshly ground black pepper

1 ounce fresh spinach

8 ounces cooked penne pasta

1 tablespoon feta cheese

1 teaspoon toasted pine nuts

Chicken

1 4-ounce chicken breast

1/4 teaspoon extra virgin olive oil

1/4 teaspoon Italian seasoning or Herbs de Provence (dried)

Chicken: Marinate the chicken and grill or sauté it. Cool and slice or dice to your desired size. Set aside.

Pasta: Heat the oil in a pan, then add mushrooms, garlic, chicken, and sun-dried tomatoes sautéing lightly. Next, add the basil, chicken stock, feta, and let thicken. Adjust the seasonings, if desired, then add the spinach and pasta and toss to wilt. Top with feta and pine nuts and serve.

Serving size: 1/2 recipe

Yields: 2 servings

Nutrition Facts (per serving): 479 calories, 20g total fat, 4g saturated fat, 384mg sodium, 49g carbohydrates, 6g fiber.

Healthy Living Tip

When choosing whole wheat pasta, look at the fiber content on the food label. Choose a product that has at least 3 grams of fiber per serving.

Chicken with Gorgonzola and Walnut Sauce

4 4-ounce chicken breasts, skinless, boneless

1 garlic clove, crushed

1/3 cup parsley leaves, roughly chopped

2 tablespoons rosemary, chopped

1 tablespoon chopped walnuts

1/4 cup extra virgin olive oil

2 tablespoons walnut oil

2 ounces gorgonzola cheese, crumbled

1 tablespoon Parmesan cheese, grated

salt and pepper to taste

Sauce: Put the garlic, parsley, rosemary, walnuts and both oils in a food processor and process until fairly smooth. Add the cheeses and process again, then season to taste with salt and pepper. Grill the chicken on medium-high heat until done. Once chicken is grilled, top with the walnut cheese sauce. Any remaining sauce can be stored in a sealed container for up to 5 days.

Serving size: 1 chicken breast with sauce

Yields: 4 servings

Nutrition Facts (per serving): 317 calories, 21g total fat, 4.8g saturated fat, 271mg sodium, 1g carbohydrates, 0g fiber.

Healthy Living Tip

This recipe contains a moderate amount of natural fat from the walnut oil, nuts and cheese. Nuts are a good source of monounsaturated fat. Cheese with strong flavors, such as bleu cheese and Parmesan, offer more flavor with a lesser amount of cheese.

Citrus Grilled Salmon

1 teaspoon lemon zest

2 tablespoons fresh lemon juice

2 tablespoons agave nectar

4 teaspoons chili powder

1 teaspoon ground cumin

1/4 teaspoon ground red pepper

1 cup orange juice

4 4-ounce salmon fillets, skin off

1 pinch sea salt

1 pinch black pepper, freshly ground

non-stick cooking spray

Combine the lemon zest, lemon juice, agave nectar, chili powder, cumin, red pepper and orange juice in a bowl as a marinade. In a separate bowl, add two ounces of the marinade to the fish, then toss well and set aside to marinate for one hour. Place remaining orange mixture in a small saucepan and bring it to a simmer and cook until reduced by a third. You should have about 4 ounces of marinade. Season the fish with salt and pepper, then place the fish on a preheated grill coated with cooking spray. Grill for 7 minutes per side until fish flakes easily when tested with a fork. Serve with reduced marinade.

Serving size: 1 salmon fillet

Yields: 4 servings

Nutrition Facts (per serving): 366 calories, 13g total fat, 2g saturated fat, 210mg sodium, 27g carbohydrates, 1g fiber, *Gluten-Free*

Healthy Living Tip

A serving of salmon is a rich source of omega-3 fatty acids which has been shown to increase good cholesterol (HDL) and prevent heart disease.

If grilling with the skin on salmon, cook the skin side first for seven minutes. Flip and the skin will peel off easily with a pair of tongs.

Diet Dr. Pepper Marinated Pork Loin

1 cup Diet Dr. Pepper

1 cup red wine vinegar

1 large rosemary branch, about 4-6 inches long

1/2 teaspoon whole black peppercorns

2 large cloves garlic, peeled and crushed

2 sprigs thyme

2 pounds pork loin, natural or organic for less sodium

Kosher salt to taste

freshly ground black pepper

To make the marinade combine the Dr. Pepper and red wine vinegar in a mixing bowl. Lightly crush the rosemary and the black peppercorns, then add them with the garlic and thyme to the mixing bowl. Trim the pork and place it in a large zip-top bag adding the marinade. Carefully squeeze out as much air as possible so the meat is submerged in the marinade. Place the bag on a plate or in a pan, in case the bag leaks. Refrigerate the loin overnight. Preheat oven to 350F degrees. Roast the loin for 30-45 minutes or until 160F degrees internal temperature and allow to rest for 5 minutes before slicing.

Serving size: 4 ounces

Yields: 6 servings

Nutrition Facts (per serving): 236 calories, 12g total fat, 4g saturated fat, 44mg sodium, 0g carbohydrates, 0g fiber, *Gluten-Free*

Healthy Living Tip

Most soft drink marinades use full sugar versions because of the caramelizing of the sugar, but this recipe gives the pork a great flavor without the added sugar.

Flank Steak Fajitas

1 pound flank steak, trimmed

1 bottle Mrs. Dash Mesquite Grille 10-minute Marinade

1 teaspoon olive oil

3/4 cup julienne yellow onions

1/2 cup julienne red pepper

1/2 cup julienne yellow squash

1/2 cup julienne zucchini

3/4 cup sliced crimini mushrooms

8 six-inch tortillas, plain, whole wheat or flavored

Add 3/4 cup of Mrs. Dash marinade to the meat and let it marinate for 10 minutes. Remove the meat and discard the remaining marinade. Preheat the grill to medium-high heat, and grill the flank steak to desired doneness. Allow the meat to rest for 3-4 minutes before slicing. Cut the meat diagonally across the grain into thin strips and keep it warm. Grill vegetables on aluminum foil over the grill until tender or sauté them in a preheated pan. Drizzle additional marinade over vegetables while cooking. Arrange the beef and vegetables on a serving platter. Warm the tortillas by wrapping them in foil and placing them on grill. Serve with healthier fajita toppings listed below.

Serving size: 2 fajitas

Yields: 4 servings

Nutrition Facts (per serving): 350 calories, 10g total fat, 3g saturated fat, 250mg sodium, 35g carbohydrates, 4g fiber.

Healthy Living Tip

Choose from the following healthier fajita toppings: fat-free sour cream, no-added-salt canned tomatoes, salsa, fresh chopped cilantro, fresh sliced avocado, reduced-fat cheese, or black beans.

Garlic Herb Chicken Skewers

1 tablespoon olive oil

1 teaspoon garlic

1 teaspoon fresh thyme

1 teaspoon fresh basil

1 teaspoon paprika

Kosher salt to taste

4 3-ounce chicken breasts

4 wooden or metal skewers (soak wooden skewers in water overnight)

Combine ingredients and marinate the chicken for 4 hours. Dice the chicken into 1-inch, uniform pieces and skewer. Grill them over medium-high heat until the internal temperature is 165F degrees.

Serving size: 1 chicken skewer

Yields: 4 servings

Nutrition Facts (per serving): 175 calories, 6g total fat, 1g saturated fat, 134mg sodium, 1g carbohydrates, 0g fiber, *Gluten-Free*

Healthy Living Tip

Healthy protein options for grilling: chicken or turkey breast, pork loin, ground sirloin or 93% lean ground turkey, fish or shrimp, sirloin steak, flank steak, or beef tenderloin, Portobello mushrooms, mixed vegetables or tofu.

Grilled Flank Steak with Balsamic Caramelized Onions

¼ cup balsamic vinegar

1 tablespoon olive oil

6 cups julienne yellow onions

1/2 teaspoon salt, divided

1 pound flank steak, trimmed

1/4 teaspoon freshly ground black pepper

1/2 teaspoon fresh rosemary, chopped

non-stick cooking spray

Heat the oil in a large non-stick skillet over medium-high heat. Add the onion, and sauté for 10 minutes or until tender. Sprinkle with 1/4 teaspoon salt and sauté 15 minutes more or until the onions are golden brown. If the onions start to get too dark or the pan starts to burn, add a little water to slow the cooking down. Add the balsamic vinegar and simmer for three minutes, then remove from the heat. Preheat the grill and coat the grill rack with pan spray. Sprinkle the steak with the remaining 1/4 teaspoon of salt, pepper, and rosemary. Grill the steak for 6 minutes on each side or until desired doneness. Cut the steak diagonally across the grain into thin slices. Garnish the steak with onions.

Serving size: 3 ounces

Yields: 4 servings

Nutrition Facts (per serving): 302 calories, 10g total fat, 3g saturated fat, 360mg sodium, 29g carbohydrates, 3g fiber, ***Gluten-Free***

Grilled Halibut with Corn Sauté

1/2 tablespoon olive oil

2 4-ounce halibut fillets

1/4 cup julienne yellow onion

1 tablespoon garlic clove, minced

1/4 cup fresh yellow corn kernels

1-2 Roma tomatoes, diced

3 ounces fresh green beans, trimmed and blanched

2 tablespoons white wine

1 tablespoon tarragon, fresh chopped

Kosher salt and ground pepper to taste

Preheat the oven to 350F degrees. Preheat a large sauté pan over medium-high heat, then add the oil. Once the oil is hot, add the fish and sear the top of the fillet for about 3 minutes until it's golden brown. Flip the fish and place the pan in the oven and cook for 5-6 minutes or until done. In a separate pan, add garlic, onions, corn and sauté for two minutes. Add the green beans and tomatoes, then sauté for two minutes more. Deglaze with wine, season with tarragon, then salt and pepper to taste. Remove the fish from the oven and place on two plates. Top with vegetables.

Serving size: 1/2 recipe

Yields: 2 servings

Nutrition Facts (per serving): 354 calories, 11.5g total fat, 1g saturated fat, 330mg sodium, 14g carbohydrates, 3g fiber, *Gluten-Free*

Healthy Living Tip

As with most of our recipes, many other proteins can be good with this dish. If you do not have halibut, try another whitefish. You can also substitute chicken or pork!

Honey Rosemary Roasted Turkey Breast

4 pounds turkey breast

2 tablespoons honey

2 tablespoons fresh chopped rosemary

1/2 tablespoon black pepper

1/2 teaspoon garlic powder

1/2 teaspoon onion powder

1/2 teaspoon salt

Mix the honey, rosemary, pepper, powders and salt, then rub the entire turkey breast with this mixture. Bake the turkey at 350F degrees for 1 1/2 to 2 hours. Check the internal temperature making sure that it is at least 165F degrees. Slice and serve with Cranberry-Apple Relish.

Serving size: 3 ounces

Yields: 12 servings

Nutrition Facts (per serving): 100 calories, 3g total fat, 0g saturated fat, 50mg sodium, 3g carbohydrates, 0g fiber, *Gluten-Free*

Healthy Living Tip

Try this recipe for a holiday meal entrée. The marinade can be used for pork tenderloin as well. Rosemary has a wonderful smell and contains substances that aid digestion and improve the immune system.

Israeli Couscous with Chicken and Asparagus

Chicken

4 tablespoons extra virgin olive oil

2 tablespoons fresh lemon juice

1 teaspoon minced garlic

1/2 teaspoon lemon zest

18 ounces chicken breast, sliced

Couscous

1 cup whole wheat couscous

1 1/2 cups low-sodium chicken broth or vegetable broth

Vegetables

2 teaspoons garlic clove, minced

2 1/2 cups asparagus spears, blanched and cut diagonally into 3/4-inch pieces

1 cup julienne red onion

1 cup green peas

2 ounces white wine

1/3 cup chopped fresh chives

1/4 cup Parmesan cheese, grated

Whisk 2 tablespoons of the oil, lemon juice, garlic, and lemon zest in a small bowl. Add sliced chicken and allow it to marinate for at least two hours. In a preheated large sauté pan, add the oil and once hot, add the couscous. Sauté for a minute and add broth. Bring to a boil, then reduce to a simmer and cover for about 10 minutes until all the liquid is absorbed. If it is too dry, you can add more broth a little at a time. In a preheated, large sauté pan, add the oil and when oil is hot, add chicken. Cook the chicken until 3/4 done, then add the garlic, asparagus, red onion and peas. Sauté for about 3 minutes until it's lightly tender but still firm in the middle. Deglaze with wine and simmer for 30 seconds to allow the alcohol to burn off, then add the couscous, chives and cheese. Season with salt and pepper and toss.

Serving size: 1/6 recipe

Yields: 6 servings

Nutrition Facts (per serving): 390 calories, 13g total fat, 3g saturated fat, 253mg sodium, 38g carbohydrates, 5g fiber.

Healthy Living Tip

There are two types of couscous. Israeli is more of a quick cooking couscous that can have hot liquid added to it and will absorb it in a covered bowl. Pearl is larger pasta that requires cooking over heat like rice. You will need to read the cooking directions on the packet and adapt accordingly.

Oven Fried Garlic Chicken

4 4-ounce chicken breasts, skinless, boneless

2 cups cornflake cereal

1/4 cup egg substitute

1 teaspoon garlic powder

1/2 teaspoon salt

1/2 teaspoon pepper

1 teaspoon parsley flakes

1 tablespoon chili powder

Preheat oven to 425F degrees. Coat a 13 x 9-inch baking dish with a light layer of vegetable or olive oil. Put the cornflakes into a large plastic bag and crush them using a rolling pin until the cornflakes resemble coarse bread crumbs. Add the garlic powder, salt, pepper, parsley, and chili powder and shake the bag until the ingredients are well mixed. Place egg substitute in a small bowl and coat the chicken breast, then place in the bag with the cornflake mixture. Shake the bag until the chicken breast is covered, then place it in the baking dish. Repeat this step with the remaining chicken breasts. Place the baking dish in the oven and bake for 45 minutes. Let it cool for 5 minutes before eating.

Serving size: 1 piece of chicken

Yields: 4 servings

Nutrition Facts (per serving): 253 calories, 3g total fat, 1g saturated fat, 286mg sodium, 17g carbohydrates, 1g fiber.

Healthy Living Tip

This recipe gives you a crisp coating with lots of flavor without the fat that comes with fried chicken.

Poached Salmon

1/2 cup white wine

1/2 cup lemon juice

1 teaspoon capers, drained

1 teaspoon dill

1/4 teaspoon white pepper

1 tablespoon lemon zest

1 bay leaf

2 4-ounce salmon fillets

Mix all ingredients (except the salmon) in large saucepan, then heat on medium-high heat until the liquid starts to boil. Pour the liquid into a roasting pan or a deep baking dish. Add the salmon fillets, then place the dish in a preheated oven on 350F degrees. Cook 10-12 minutes or until the fish flakes. Remove the fish from the liquid and serve.

Serving size: 1 piece of salmon

Yields: 2 servings

Nutrition Facts (per serving): 175 calories, 7g total fat, 1g saturated fat, 50mg sodium, 0g carbohydrates, 0g fiber, *Gluten-Free*

Healthy Living Tip

The American Heart Association recommends eating a 3 ounce portion of fish 2-3 times per week. Poaching is a quick and healthy cooking method that infuses flavor into fish without adding extra fat.

Quinoa Chicken Picatta

8 ounces chicken breast, skinless, boneless

2 tablespoons quinoa flour

2 teaspoons olive oil

2 tablespoons white wine

2 tablespoons fresh lemon juice

¼ cup low-sodium chicken stock

1 teaspoon cornstarch

2 tablespoons capers, drained

2 tablespoons parsley, chopped

salt and pepper to taste

Use either two or four ounce breasts, or cut one eight ounce breast into two filets. Place the chicken between two pieces of plastic wrap and lightly pound to 1/4-inch thickness. Place the quinoa flour in a shallow baking dish, then dip the chicken into the flour to coat; shake off any excess. Heat the olive oil in a heavy large skillet, then add the chicken and cook for about three minutes on both sides until golden brown and cooked through. Transfer to a platter and set aside. Heat two tablespoons of oil over medium heat in a large sauté pan, then add the chicken breasts and cook until golden brown, about two minutes per side. Transfer to a platter and set aside. Be careful not to have the pan too hot or the outside of the chicken will burn. Using the same pan, add the wine and deglaze the pan. Add lemon juice and cold stock mixed with cornstarch, then bring to a simmer and allow to thicken. Add the capers and parsley, then season with salt and pepper. Pour over the chicken and serve.

Serving size: 1/2 recipe

Yields: 2 servings

Nutrition Facts (per serving): 193 calories, 6g total fat, 1g saturated fat, 407mg sodium, 11g carbohydrates, 1g fiber, *Gluten-Free*

Healthy Living Tip

By using quinoa flour this dish becomes gluten-free. Quinoa flour has more protein and fewer carbohydrates than wheat flour.

Quinoa Stir Fry with Chicken

3/4 cup quinoa, rinsed

1/4 teaspoon Kosher salt

1 tablespoon canola oil

4 ounces julienne yellow onion

4 ounces julienne red pepper

4 ounces carrots, diagonally sliced

2 teaspoons ginger, minced

4 teaspoons garlic clove, minced

1 dried red chili (optional)

2 cups snow peas, trimmed

1/4 teaspoon black pepper, freshly ground

12 ounces chicken breast, skinless, boneless, 1/2-inch diced

1 ounce gluten-free soy sauce

2 green onion, sliced

2 tablespoons cilantro, chopped

1/4 cup basil, chiffonade

Place quinoa in a small saucepan with water and salt. Bring to a boil, then reduce the heat to low. Cover and cook about 15 minutes until the quinoa absorbs the water. Remove from heat, fluff with a fork and leave uncovered. Add canola oil to a preheated large sauté pan, then add the chicken and cook for about 3 minutes to 3/4 done. Add the garlic and ginger, onions, red peppers and dried chili, sauté for about two minutes, leave firm. Add peas and season with pepper, then cook for another minute. Add the soy sauce and quinoa and cook until hot. Finish with green onions and herbs.

Serving size: 1/4 recipe

Yields: 4 servings

Nutrition Facts (per serving): 367 calories, 9g total fat, 1g saturated fat, 394mg sodium, 36g carbohydrates, 7g fiber, **Gluten-Free**

Healthy Living Tip

Beef or shrimp works great with this dish as well. For a gluten free version, check the ingredient label on the soy sauce. Most have wheat as a main ingredient but there are wheat-free brands in most stores.

How to chiffonade basil: pick fresh basil leaves from the stem and stack one on top of another, then roll into a cigar shape. Cut into 1/8-inch wide ribbon cuts.

Tuscan Fish

4 4-ounce skinless cod or other whitefish fillets

1 tablespoon extra virgin olive oil

1 medium onion, thinly sliced

2 cups Roma tomatoes, diced

1/4 cup Kalamata olives, pitted and sliced

1 teaspoon fresh thyme

1 teaspoon capers, drained

In a small saucepan, heat the oil over medium heat, then add the onion and garlic, sauté until tender. Add the tomatoes, olives, thyme, and capers and simmer, uncovered, for 10 minutes, or until most of the liquid has evaporated. Preheat the broiler and spray an unheated rack of a broiler pan with cooking spray. Place the fish on the rack, tucking under any thin edges. Broil 3-4 inches from heat for 4-6 minutes per 1-2 inch thickness or until fish flakes easily, turning once if fillets are 1 inch thick. Top with sauce and serve.

Serving size: 1 fish fillet

Yields: 4 servings

Nutrition Facts (per serving): 162 calories, 5g total fat, 1g saturated fat, 250mg sodium, 7g carbohydrates, 2g fiber, *Gluten-Free*

Healthy Living Tip

This is a great example of how people eat in the Mediterranean region. It has fish, olive oil, olives, and vegetables. To continue Mediterranean diet recommendations, pair with a whole grain source such as whole wheat pasta or couscous.

Yogurt Marinated Chicken

1 cup low-fat or non-fat plain yogurt

juice from 1 fresh lime

2 cloves garlic

2 tablespoons honey

1/4 cup minced red onion

2 tablespoons cilantro, chopped

4 4-ounce skinless, boneless chicken breasts

Mix all the ingredients except the chicken in a large bowl. Add the chicken to the mixture and coat. Cover the bowl and refrigerate overnight or for at least 4 hours. Preheat the grill. Remove the chicken from the marinade and discard the marinade. Sprinkle the chicken with salt (optional) and pepper. Place the chicken on the hot grill and cook until the juices run clear, 6-8 minutes per side. Serve with the Fresh Corn Salsa recipe.

Serving size: 1 piece of chicken

Yields: 4 servings

Nutrition Facts (per serving): 200 calories, 2g total fat, 0g saturated fat, 122mg sodium, 6g carbohydrates, 0g fiber, *Gluten-Free*

Healthy Living Tip

Never reuse any liquid that meat has been marinating in to avoid cross contamination of bacteria.

Sandwiches, Soups, and Entree Salads

Featured: Chipotle Portobello Sandwich and Seared Salmon with Tomato, Cucumber, Mint and Parsley Salad

Asian Tuna Wrap

Wrap

1 pound fresh tuna, preferably albacore

1 pound baby spinach (can substitute lettuce)

2 cups cherry tomatoes halved

1 cup Mandarin oranges

4 twelve-inch tortillas, plain, whole wheat or flavored

non-stick cooking spray

Dressing

2 cups plain yogurt

3 tablespoons rice wine vinegar

2 teaspoons minced ginger root (or substitute 1/2 teaspoon dried ginger)

1 tablespoon light soy sauce

1 tablespoon fresh lime juice

1 tablespoon lime zest

2 tablespoons orange juice

2 tablespoons orange zest

2 tablespoons brown sugar

1/2 teaspoon crushed red pepper (optional)

Mix ingredients for dressing, refrigerate until needed. Brush tuna lightly with oil or use a cooking spray. Grill the tuna to desired doneness (tuna can be cooked anywhere from medium rare to well done, depending on preference). Chill and slice into 1/4-inch wide strips. To assemble wraps place a tortilla on a flat, dry surface. Spread about 2 tablespoons of dressing on the tortilla. Layer in order: 2 cups loose fresh spinach (or lettuce), 4 ounces tuna, 1/2 cup tomatoes, 1/4 cup Mandarin oranges. Drizzle another tablespoon of dressing across the top. Fold bottom of the wrap over the filling; fold each side in overlapping the bottom fold about 2 inches on both sides. Roll the pocket of filling up to make a burrito style wrap. Cut completed wrap on the bias (at an angle) and serve with extra dressing.

Serving size: 1 wrap

Yields: 4 servings

Nutrition Facts (per serving): 259 calories, 3g total fat, 1g saturated fat, 278mg sodium, 26g carbohydrates, 3g fiber.

Healthy Living Tip

This recipe contains many healthy nutrient sources: Spinach is a superfood packed with iron and vitamin K. Ginger is beneficial to the digestive system. Tuna is an omega-3 fatty acid source.

Barbecue Chicken Wrap with Jicama Slaw

8 ounces Jicama Slaw

2 ounces Carolina Barbecue Sauce

1 pound cooked chicken breast, cut into 1/2-inch cubes

4 six-inch tortillas

This wrap uses the sauce from the Carolina Barbecue Pork Sandwiches recipe. To assemble the wrap, place the tortilla on flat dry surface. Spread the barbecue sauce on the tortilla and layer the chicken and jicama slaw. Jicama Slaw recipe on following page. Wrap burrito style by folding the bottom of wrap over the filling; fold each side in overlapping the bottom fold about 2 inches on both sides. Roll the pocket of filling up to make a burrito style wrap. Cut completed wrap on the bias (at an angle) and serve with sauce.

Serving size: 1 wrap

Yields: 4 servings

Nutrition Facts (per serving): 307 calories, 6g total fat, 1.5g saturated fat, 600mg sodium, 32g carbohydrates, 2g fiber.

Jicama Slaw

1 red onion, minced

1/4 teaspoon salt

¼ cup extra virgin olive oil

2 1/2 tablespoons lime juice

1 teaspoon sugar

1/4 teaspoon black pepper, freshly ground

2 1/2 pounds jicama, peeled and julienne

1/3 cup fresh chopped cilantro

Whisk the lime juice, oil, sugar, pepper, and remaining 3/4 teaspoon salt in a large bowl until combined well. Add the onion, jicama, cilantro, and salt to taste and toss well.

Serving size: 1/2 cup

Yields: 16 servings

Nutrition Facts (per serving): 62 calories, 4g total fat, 1g saturated fat, 21mg sodium, 7g carbohydrates, 4g fiber, *Gluten-Free*

Healthy Living Tip

Jicama is a root vegetable that is crisp and slightly sweet. The outer brown peel must be removed before eating. Unlike a potato it can be eaten raw. Jicama is high in vitamin C and magnesium.

Black Bean Veggie Sliders

2 cups black beans, drained

1 1/2 cups cooked brown rice

1/8 cup toasted walnuts

1/4 cup roasted red peppers

1 cup yellow onion, diced

1 bunch cilantro, chopped

3 tablespoons basil, chopped

1/8 cup fresh lemon juice

5 cloves garlic, roasted

1/2 habanero pepper, seeded and chopped (optional)

1 tablespoon cumin

2 tablespoons paprika

1 tablespoon olive oil

salt and pepper to taste

Rough chop all the ingredients in a food processor. Portion the mixture into 2 ounce patties. In a hot skillet add olive oil, then add the patties and brown on both sides about 2-3 minutes a side. Serve with whole wheat slider buns. Top with salsa and low-fat cheese if desired.

Serving size: 1 slider

Yields: 10 servings

Nutrition Facts (per serving): 200 calories, 3g total fat, <1g saturated fat, 250mg sodium, 34g carbohydrates, 8g fiber.

Healthy Living Tip

Eating a meatless meal is a great way to reduce your daily saturated fat intake and can increase your fiber intake. Black beans are a great source of protein and fiber. Simply draining and rinsing the beans reduces the sodium content by about 30%.

Carolina Pork Barbecue Sandwiches

Barbecue Pork

2 pounds pork loin, natural or organic for less sodium

3 onions, sliced

1/2 cup barbecue sauce (see recipe following)

8 whole grain buns

Carolina Barbecue Sauce

1 cup cider vinegar

1/2 cup low-sodium ketchup

3 tablespoons packed brown sugar

1 tablespoon Worcestershire sauce

1/2 teaspoon black pepper

1/2 teaspoon white pepper

Barbecue Pork: Place the meat in a slow cooker; top with onions and sauce. Cover with a lid and cook on low for 8-10 hours or on high for 4-5 hours. Remove the meat from slow cooker and remove any excess fat. Shred the meat using 2 forks or chop the meat into small pieces. Return the meat to the slow cooker. Stir until evenly coated with barbecue sauce. Fill buns with meat mixture before serving.

Barbecue Sauce: Combine all the ingredients in a medium saucepan and bring to a boil over medium heat. Reduce the heat and simmer for 20 minutes, stirring frequently. Remove from heat and cool slightly before using. Makes 1 1/2 cups.

Serving size: 1 sandwich (3 ounces meat, 2 tablespoons sauce, and whole wheat bun)

Yields: 8 sandwiches

Nutrition Facts (per serving): 294 calories, 11g total fat, 4g saturated fat, 300mg sodium, 28g carbohydrates, 3g fiber.

Healthy Living Tip

A traditional barbecue sauce has an average of 424 mg of sodium per serving, which is 41% higher in sodium than this recipe. Maintaining a 2,400 mg sodium diet is recommended to manage blood pressure for overall heart health.

Chipotle Portobello Sandwich

4 medium Portobello mushrooms

4 leaves green leaf lettuce

2 roasted red peppers (fresh or jarred)

4 whole wheat sandwich buns

1 12-ounce bottle, Mrs. Dash Southwestern - Chipotle 10 Minute Marinade

1 cup fat-free sour cream

non-stick cooking spray, as needed

Marinate the mushrooms in one half of the Mrs. Dash for at least 30 minutes. Discard the used marinade. Grill the mushrooms on medium-high heat for about 3 to 4 minutes per side. Mix two tablespoons of the Mrs. Dash to the sour cream and hold cold until ready for assembly of the sandwich. Layer the bottom bun with one tablespoon of the sour cream chipotle sauce, one leaf of green leaf lettuce, one grilled Portobello mushroom, roasted red pepper and one more tablespoon of the sour cream chipotle sauce. Top with the other half of the bun and serve.

Serving size: 1 sandwich

Yields: 4 servings

Nutrition Facts (per serving): 196 calories, 3g total fat, 1g saturated fat, 320mg sodium, 34g carbohydrates, 6g fiber.

Healthy Living Tip

To roast fresh red peppers: spray peppers with cooking spray and grill until charred. Place peppers in a zip-top bag and let them sweat for about 10 minutes. Take the peppers out and remove the skin and seeds and separate into four equal pieces.

Grilled Shrimp Salad with Roasted Garlic Balsamic Vinaigrette

Salad

1/2 pound asparagus, blanched

8 cups Romaine lettuce, chopped

1/2 cup red pepper, julienne

1 cup Portobello mushrooms, sliced

1/4 cup black olives

2 ounces sliced almonds, toasted

Shrimp skewer

1 pound shrimp (16-20 count)

4 wooden skewers, pre-soaked

1/2 tablespoon extra virgin olive oil

1 teaspoon garlic clove, chopped

salt and freshly ground black pepper to taste

4 tablespoons Parmesan cheese, grated

Blanch the asparagus in lightly salted boiling water for 2-4 minutes depending on size of spears, until they are bright green and firm but not crunchy in the middle. Immediately shock in ice water to stop the cooking. Place salad greens in four separate bowls for serving. Add each vegetable, arranging in groups. Add grilled shrimp skewer. Serve Roasted Garlic Vinaigrette on the side. Vinaigrette recipe on following page.

Serving size: 1 portion salad and shrimp skewer with 2 tablespoons vinaigrette

Yields: 4 servings

Nutrition Facts (per serving): 346 calories, 20g total fat, 2.5g saturated fat, 372mg sodium, 16.5g carbohydrates, 5.5g fiber, *Gluten-Free*

Roasted Garlic Balsamic Vinaigrette

1 cup extra virgin olive oil

1/2 cup balsamic vinegar

2 tablespoons garlic, roasted

1 tablespoon parsley, fresh chopped

1 tablespoon oregano, fresh chopped

1 tablespoon thyme, fresh chopped

1 tablespoon honey

Preheat oven to 375F degrees. Cut top of garlic head off to make a flat surface and place in the bottom of a small roasting pan and cover with foil. Roast for 30-45 minutes or until soft and able to squeeze the garlic out of the skin. Place all the ingredients in a blender or food processor except for the oil. Turn on and add oil in a slow stream until incorporated.

Serving size: 2 tablespoons

Yields: 1 ½ cups

Nutrition Facts (per serving): 104 calories, 10g total fat, 1g saturated fat, 30mg sodium, 4g carbohydrates, 0g fiber, *Gluten-Free*

Herb Roasted Pork Loin Sandwich with Balsamic Marinated Mushrooms

1 pound pork loin	2 tablespoons onion, finely diced
1/2 tablespoon olive oil	1 1/2 teaspoons garlic cloves, finely chopped
1/2 teaspoon Kosher salt	2 teaspoons Dijon mustard
1/2 teaspoon black pepper	5 whole wheat buns
1/2 teaspoon rosemary, chopped	2 tablespoons Dijon mustard
1/2 teaspoon thyme, crushed	1 tablespoon fresh basil, chopped
1/2 teaspoon oregano, chopped	Balsamic Marinated Mushrooms

Preheat oven to 250F degrees with a rack in the middle. Pat the pork dry and season with half the salt and pepper. Sear the pork on all sides in a preheated non-stick skillet. Stir together the shallots, garlic, mustard, herbs and 1 tablespoon of oil and smear over the top and sides of roast, then put roast, fat side up, in a roasting pan with a rack in the bottom. Roast at 250F degrees for 2-3 hours, or until pork is fork tender. Let rest and pull apart by hand or using a carving fork. Prepare the basil mustard by mixing 2 tablespoons Dijon mustard and 1 tablespoon fresh chopped basil. Assemble sandwich by placing 3 ounces of pork on the bottom bun, top with 1/2 slice Portobello mushroom and spread 1/2 tablespoon basil mustard on the top bun. Balsamic Marinated Mushrooms recipe on following page.

Serving size: 1 sandwich

Yields: 5 servings

Nutrition Facts (per serving): 325 calories, 12g total fat, 1.5g saturated fat, 564mg sodium, 28g carbohydrates, 4g fiber.

Balsamic Marinated Mushrooms

3 Portobello mushrooms

2 tablespoons olive oil

1 tablespoon balsamic vinegar

2 cloves garlic, chopped

In a small bowl, mix together the oil, vinegar and garlic. Remove stems from the mushroom caps and coat well with dressing. Roast at 350F degrees for 12-15 minutes or until soft. Allow to cool before slicing.

Serving size: 1/5 recipe

Yields: 5 servings

Nutrition Facts (per serving): 65 calories, 6g total fat, <1g saturated fat, 4mg sodium, 3g carbohydrates, 1g fiber, *Gluten-Free*

Mexican Quiche Pie

Shell Ingredients

1 white corn tortilla

1/4 teaspoon olive oil

Filling Ingredients

1 egg

1/2 cup shredded Monterey Jack cheese

1 tablespoon milk

1 tablespoon chopped yellow onion

2 teaspoons canned diced green chilies

1 teaspoon diced pimiento, drained

salt and pepper to taste

For Crust: Use mini tart baking pans for the forms. Heat the oven to 350F degrees and brush one side of the tortilla with oil and one side with water, then place on a microwaveable dish and microwave for 20 seconds for one tortilla. Remove tortilla from the microwave and with the oil side down, press into a mini tart pan. Place a second tart pan on top of the tortilla and press firmly into form. With the tortilla sandwiched between mini tart pans, bake shell for 3 minutes. Remove inserted tart pan, exposing shell that now holds its shape, and finish baking shell for 2 additional minutes. Either cool the shells and store or fill with egg mixture and bake.

Egg filling: Mix together all the ingredients and pour into shells. Bake for 10-15 minutes or until egg mix is just firm.

Serving size: 1 quiche

Nutrition Facts (per serving): 382 calories, 27g total fat, 14g saturated fat, 571mg sodium, 14g carbohydrates, 2g fiber, *Gluten-Free*

Healthy Living Tip

This recipe is from Janet Prince's book, *My Gluten-Free Knoxville*. Depending on the size of egg and depth of your finished shell, you may need one or two additional shells to hold any left-over filling. Make a few extra shells to hold condiments, such as chopped olives.

Seared Salmon with Tomato, Cucumber, Mint, and Parsley Salad

Salad

3 medium fresh ripe red tomatoes

1/2 cucumber, quartered lengthwise and finely sliced

1/2 cup spring mix

2 scallions, including most of the green, thinly sliced

1 cup fresh-flat-leaf parsley, tightly packed, coarsely chopped

3 tablespoons fresh mint leaves, chopped

1 tablespoon fresh thyme, chopped

2 tablespoons capers, rinsed well and drained (optional)

Dressing

3 tablespoons extra virgin olive oil

1 tablespoon fresh lemon juice

1 tablespoon balsamic vinegar

2 teaspoons grated lemon zest

salt and freshly ground black pepper

Salmon

4 4-ounce salmon fillets

1 1/2 tablespoons fresh lemon juice

1 1/2 tablespoons olive oil

salt and freshly ground black pepper to taste

Salad: Cut the tomatoes in half, crosswise and squeeze lightly to remove the seeds. With a serrated knife, dice the tomatoes and transfer to a strainer to drain. In a salad bowl, mix together the cucumber, greens, scallions, herbs, and capers. Add the tomatoes.

Dressing: Whisk the olive oil, lemon juice, vinegar, and lemon zest together and salt and pepper to taste, then pour over the salad and toss. Taste and adjust the seasonings. Refrigerate for 20-30 minutes to give the flavors time to meld. Divide among four plates for service.

Salmon: Place salmon fillets in a shallow bowl. Toss well with lemon juice, olive oil, salt and pepper. Let rest for 15 minutes. Cook the salmon in a non-stick sauté pan about 3-4 minutes a side, searing on both sides until done. Place on the salad and serve.

Serving size: 1 salad

Yields: 4 servings

Nutrition Facts (per serving): 115 calories, 9g total fat, 1g saturated fat, 75mg sodium, 6g carbohydrates, 3g fiber, **Gluten-Free**

Summertime Salad with Grilled Chicken and Strawberry Vinaigrette

8 cups mixed greens

1 cup cucumber, diced

1 cup cherry tomatoes, halved

1 cup jicama, sliced

1/2 cup red onion

2 ounces feta cheese, crumbled

2 ounces pecans, chopped

12 ounces diced grilled chicken breast

Place salad greens in a large bowl. Add remaining dry ingredients and toss. Drizzle with Strawberry Vinaigrette (2 tablespoons per serving). Vinaigrette recipe on following page.

Serving size: 1/4 salad recipe and 2 tablespoons vinaigrette

Yields: 4 servings

Nutrition Facts (per serving): 416 calories, 27g total fat, 5g saturated fat, 277mg sodium, 15g carbohydrates, 4.5g fiber, *Gluten-Free*

Strawberry Vinaigrette

1/2 cup grapeseed oil

1/4 cup red wine vinegar

1 cup strawberries, sliced (reserve 2 ounces)

1 garlic clove, minced

1 tablespoon honey

1 pinch salt and freshly ground black pepper

Add all ingredients to blender except oil and reserved strawberries. Blend on medium and slowly add oil in a steady stream until incorporated. Place in serving dish and add reserved strawberries.

Serving Size: 2 tablespoons

Yields: 1 ½ cups

Nutrition Facts (per serving): 105 calories, 11g total fat, 1g saturated fat, 30mg sodium, 3g carbohydrates, 0g fiber, *Gluten-Free*

White Chicken Chili

1 pound skinless, boneless chicken breasts, cut into bite-sized pieces

1 teaspoon olive oil

1 large onion, chopped

1 tablespoon garlic, minced

1 15-ounce can Great Northern beans, rinsed and drained

1 15-ounce can navy beans, rinsed and drained

1 4-ounce can chopped green chilies, drained

1 1/2 teaspoons ground cumin

1/8 teaspoon chili powder

1/8 teaspoon cayenne pepper

1 teaspoon hot pepper sauce

1 teaspoon black pepper

1 14-ounce can fat-free, low-sodium chicken broth

1/2 cup shredded, low-fat mozzarella cheese

1/4 cup fat-free sour cream

Heat the oil in a stock pot over medium heat. Add onion, garlic, cumin, chili powder, cayenne pepper, and hot pepper sauce, then sauté for 5 minutes. Push onion to one side of the pan. Add chicken to the other side of the pan. Sauté the chicken for approximately 5 minutes. Drain the beans and rinse; reserve 1/2 cup of the bean liquid. Add the beans, broth, chilies, and reserved bean liquid to the chicken. Simmer about 10 minutes until the chicken is tender and cooked through, then season to taste with pepper. Serve warm. Top with cheese and sour cream.

Serving size: 1/6 recipe

Yields: 6 servings

Nutrition Facts (per serving): 290 calories, 4g total fat, 1g saturated fat, 338mg sodium, 41g carbohydrates, 10g fiber, *Gluten-Free*

Healthy Living Tip

The daily goal for fiber intake is 25-35 grams. Great Northern beans are nutrient-packed with protein, complex carbohydrates, folate, and fiber.

Grains and Starches

Featured: Sweet Potato Salad

Almond Quinoa Pilaf

1 cup quinoa

2 cups low-sodium chicken broth or vegetable broth

non-stick cooking spray

1/2 cup yellow onion, diced

1/4 cup celery, diced

1/4 cup red pepper, diced

1/2 cup roasted slivered almonds, coarsely chopped

salt and pepper to taste

1 tablespoon fresh parsley

Rinse raw quinoa under cold water, reserve. Preheat a medium stock pot over medium-high heat. Spray a non-stick sauté pan with vegetable spray. Add the onions, celery and peppers and sauté until they are translucent. Add the broth and quinoa and bring to a boil, then reduce to a strong simmer for 10-12 minutes, until all liquid is absorbed. Add almonds, salt and pepper. Garnish with parsley.

Serving size: 1/2 cup

Yields: 6 servings

Nutrition Facts (per serving): 171 calories, 10g total fat, 1g saturated fat, 200mg sodium, 16g carbohydrates, 3g fiber, *Gluten-Free*

Healthy Living Tip

Quinoa cooks much faster than rice and is higher in protein than other grains. It is also a good source of iron and magnesium. Replace rice and other grains with quinoa for greater nutritional variety.

Enlightened Macaroni and Cheese Bake

non-stick cooking spray

4 ounces dried elbow macaroni

1/2 cup reduced-fat mild cheddar cheese

1/2 cup fat-free or part-skim ricotta cheese

1/3 cup light sour cream

1/4 cup fat-free milk

1 egg white or 1/4 cup egg substitute

1 tablespoon shredded or grated low-fat Parmesan cheese

1 teaspoon Worcestershire sauce

1/4 teaspoon garlic powder

1/2 teaspoon black pepper

1/2 teaspoon Kosher salt

1 Italian plum tomato, cut in 6 slices

1 tablespoon Panko bread crumbs

1 teaspoon shredded or grated Parmesan cheese

1/2 teaspoon paprika

Preheat oven to 375F degrees. Cook the pasta according to the directions on the box. Place in a colander and drain well. Meanwhile, in a medium bowl, stir the cheddar, ricotta, sour cream, milk, egg white, 1 tablespoon Parmesan, Worcestershire sauce, garlic powder, pepper, and salt together, then stir in the pasta. Lightly spray an 8 x 8 casserole dish with vegetable oil spray. Spoon the pasta into the baking dish. Arrange the tomato slices on top. In a small bowl, stir the bread crumbs and 1 teaspoon of Parmesan together, then sprinkle over the casserole. Sprinkle paprika over the casserole and bake for 30-35 minutes, or until heated through and golden brown around the edges.

Serving size: 1/2 cup

Yields: 6 servings

Nutrition Facts (per serving): 127 calories, 1.5g total fat, <1g saturated fat, 152mg sodium, 19g carbohydrates, 2g fiber.

Healthy Living Tip

We use Dreamfields Pasta in the recipe. Due to the type of fiber in Dreamfields, it provides half the carb servings of regular pasta. Enlightened Macaroni and Cheese Bake using Dreamfields Pasta provides 8 grams of digestible carbohydrates per serving.

Fall Butternut Squash Quinoa

1 1/2 cups quinoa

3 cups vegetable stock

2 tablespoons olive oil

3 cups butternut squash, 1/2-inch cubes

2 tablespoons olive oil

1 tablespoon minced garlic

1 cup finely chopped leeks (white part only)

1 cup yellow corn kernels, thawed

1 cup medium diced red peppers

1 tablespoon julienne fresh sage

non-stick cooking spray

Cook the quinoa in water or stock according to the directions, then spread on a rimmed baking sheet to cool. Transfer to a bowl. This can be prepared one day ahead of time. Cover and chill. Preheat oven to 350F degrees. Spray a baking sheet with non-stick cooking spray. Toss squash cubes and 2 tablespoons of oil in medium bowl. Spread the squash in single layer on the prepared sheet and sprinkle with salt and pepper. Roast for about 15 minutes, just until it's tender but firm enough to hold its shape, stirring occasionally. Transfer the squash to a bowl. Cool, cover and chill. Add 2 tablespoons of olive oil in a large skillet over medium heat and sauté the garlic until lightly browned. Add leeks and 3/4 cup water and simmer until leeks are tender; about 7 minutes. Add corn and peppers and simmer for 2 minutes longer. Add the quinoa and butternut squash and simmer until heated through and liquid is absorbed, about 4 minutes. Stir in sage and season with salt and pepper.

Serving size: 1/10 recipe

Yields: 10 servings

Nutrition Facts (per serving): 192 calories, 6g total fat, <1g saturated fat, 163mg sodium, 29g carbohydrates, 3g fiber, *Gluten-Free*

Healthy Living Tip

Butternut squash will fill you up on nutrition, but not on calories because it is lower in carbohydrates and higher in fiber.

Fresh Potato Salad

1 pound red new potatoes, scrubbed

1/2 teaspoon salt

1/4 cup non-fat mayonnaise

1/2 cup non-fat sour cream

1 1/2 teaspoons Dijon mustard

1 tablespoon sweet pickle relish

1 tablespoon chopped fresh parsley

1/4 teaspoon ground white pepper

1/2 cup green onions, sliced

1/2 cup frozen edamame

1/4 cup carrot, diced

1/4 cup red bell pepper, diced

1/4 cup celery, diced

1 hard boiled omega-3 egg, chopped

In a saucepan, cover the potatoes with water, add salt and bring to a boil. Turn down the heat and boil gently for about 20 minutes until the potatoes are tender when pierced. Drain, cool, and then quarter the potatoes. Mix the mayonnaise, sour cream, mustard, and pickle relish together and toss with the potatoes. Add parsley, pepper, vegetables, and egg, then toss together thoroughly. Taste. Adjust seasonings and serve.

Serving size: 1/2 cup

Yields: 8 servings

Nutrition Facts (per serving): 94 calories, 2g total fat, 0g saturated fat, 217mg sodium, 17g carbohydrates, 3g fiber, *Gluten-Free*

Healthy Living Tip

By adding 2 cups of vegetables alongside the potatoes, overall calories and carbohydrates are reduced while increasing nutritional value.

Golden Sun Potatoes

2 cups quartered Yukon gold potatoes

1 teaspoon extra virgin olive oil

1 tablespoon whole grain mustard

1 teaspoon fresh parsley

salt and freshly ground black pepper to taste

Preheat oven to 375F degrees. Combine the ingredients and coat the potatoes with seasonings. Place coated potatoes on a greased baking pan and roast at 375F degrees for 30-45 minutes or until done.

Serving size: 1/2 cup

Yields: 4 servings

Nutrition Facts (per serving): 103 calories, 2g total fat, 0g saturated fat, 110mg sodium, 21g carbohydrates, 2g fiber, *Gluten-Free*

Healthy Living Tip

This recipe goes great with the Garlic Herb Chicken Skewer and Swiss Chard with Onion recipes. When possible, find these ingredients at your local farmers market, they are even better!

Quinoa Stuffed Roasted Tomatoes

1 cup quinoa	2 ounces sherry
2 cups vegetable broth	8 ounces shiitake mushrooms
pinch of Kosher salt	1 teaspoon Parmesan cheese, freshly grated
1 tablespoon olive oil	1/4 cup fresh basil, chopped
1/4 cup onions, finely chopped	4 tomatoes

For tomato: Use a small sharp knife to cut into the center and scoop out some of the inside of the tomato. Lightly coat the tomato with oil, then sprinkle with Kosher salt and bake at 450F degrees until the skin is slightly soft.

For stuffing: Cook quinoa in a vegetable broth for about 15 minutes until the liquid is absorbed. Heat the olive oil in a large sauté pan and add onions, cooking until translucent. Add the mushrooms and cook until deep brown. Add cooked quinoa and mix well. Add sherry and stir. If the grain sticks to the pan, add additional sherry and stir. Cover for 3 to 5 minutes, then mix in the fresh basil. Add the stuffing to the roasted tomatoes. Top with cheese. Serve immediately.

Serving size: 1 stuffed tomato

Yields: 4 servings

Nutrition Facts (per serving): 203 calories, 6g total fat, 1g saturated fat, 132mg sodium, 34g carbohydrates, 5g fiber, *Gluten-Free*

Healthy Living Tip

This recipe is packed with nutrition. Quinoa, tomatoes and mushrooms are sources of phytonutrients that may prevent some cancers and heart disease.

Roasted Vegetable and Brown Rice Salad

1 cup medium grain brown rice

2 cups water

1/2 cup zucchini, diced

1/2 cup yellow squash, diced

1/2 cup carrots, peeled and diced

1/2 cup red bell pepper, diced

8 green onions, chopped

4 ounces arugula

1/2 ounce extra virgin olive oil

3 ounces white wine vinegar

2 tablespoons chopped fresh basil

1 pinch salt

1 pinch black pepper freshly ground

Bring rice and water to a low simmer in a small covered sauce pot and cook until done, about 30 minutes. Remove from heat and chill on a sheet pan before assembling. Combine zucchini, squash, carrots and red pepper and roast in a 350F degree oven until brown around edges, about 15 minutes. Remove from heat and chill on a sheet pan before assembling. In a small bowl, whisk olive oil, vinegar, basil, salt and pepper together and set aside. Toss the rice, roasted vegetables, green onion and arugula together. Add vinaigrette and serve.

Serving size: 2/3 cup

Yields: 8 servings

Nutrition Facts (per serving): 87 calories, 2g total fat, 0g saturated fat, 48mg sodium, 15g carbohydrates, 2g fiber, *Gluten-Free*

Rosemary Roasted New Potatoes

1 tablespoon olive oil

1 tablespoon garlic clove, minced

1/2 tablespoon rosemary, chopped

2 pounds new red potatoes, quartered

salt and pepper to taste

Preheat oven to 375F degrees. In a mixing bowl, combine oil, garlic, rosemary, salt and pepper then add potatoes and toss to coat. Bake potatoes on a greased baking sheet for 30-45 minutes until they are tender and lightly browned.

Serving size: 1/2 cup

Yields: 8 servings

Nutrition Facts (per serving): 107 calories, 1.5g total fat, 0g saturated fat, 7mg sodium, 20g carbohydrates, 2g fiber, *Gluten-Free*

Healthy Living Tip

Fresh rosemary gives potatoes a wonderful flavor without adding too much sodium. Rosemary has the added benefit of improving digestion, circulation, and concentration.

Summer Grain Salad

2 cups water

1 cup quinoa

2 tablespoons olive oil

1/2 teaspoon sea salt

1/4 cup lemon juice

1/4 cup red wine vinegar

2 cloves garlic, minced

3 tomatoes, diced

1 cucumber, diced

1 cup green onions, thinly sliced

2 carrots, grated

1 cup fresh parsley, chopped

1/4 cup cilantro

Rinse raw quinoa under cold water then set aside. In a saucepan, bring water to a boil. Add the quinoa, then reduce the heat to low, cover and simmer for 10-15 minutes. Allow to cool to room temperature then fluff with a fork. Meanwhile, in a large bowl, whisk olive oil, sea salt, lemon juice, red wine vinegar, and garlic together. Add tomatoes, cucumbers, green onions, carrots, parsley, and cilantro. Stir in the cooled quinoa. Serve immediately or allow salad to marinate in the refrigerator up to overnight.

Serving size: 1/10 recipe

Yields: 10 servings

Nutrition Facts (per serving): 90 calories, 4g total fat, 5g saturated fat, 110mg sodium, 12g carbohydrates, 2g fiber, *Gluten-Free*

Healthy Living Tip

This a favorite of the Healthy Living Kitchen team because of the light, fresh flavors. Bring this dish to picnics, tailgates, or potluck dinners since there are no food safety issues with the oil and vinegar dressing.

Sweet Potato Crunch

Filling

3 sweet potatoes, peeled and mashed

3/4 cup Splenda

1/2 cup skim milk

1 tablespoon trans-free margarine

1/4 teaspoon salt

1 teaspoon vanilla extract

2 teaspoons cinnamon

2 omega-3 eggs

Topping

1/4 cup Splenda Brown Sugar Blend

2 tablespoons trans-free margarine

1/3 cup whole wheat flour

1/3 cup walnuts, chopped

Preheat oven to 350F degrees. In a large bowl, combine all filling ingredients; mix well and put into sprayed 8 x 8-inch dish. Mix the topping ingredients. Cover potato mixture with the topping and bake for 45 minutes.

Serving size: 1/2 cup

Yields: 6 servings

Nutrition Facts (per serving): 270 calories, 12g total fat, 2g saturated fat, 135mg sodium, 23g carbohydrates, 3g fiber.

Healthy Living Tip

This dish is a great example of incorporating recipe modifications without losing flavor. The Splenda, skim milk, and trans-free margarine lower the calorie content. Adding walnuts and whole wheat flour increases the nutritional value.

Sweet Potato Salad

1 tablespoon extra virgin olive oil

2 ounce red wine vinegar

1 tablespoon garlic clove, chopped

1 medium onion, cut in 1-inch pieces

1 red bell pepper, seeded and chopped

2 pounds sweet potatoes peeled and cut into 1-inch cubes

2 ounces green onion, sliced

1/2 teaspoon thyme, crushed

salt and pepper to taste

Roast sweet potatoes in 350F degree oven for 45 minutes or until just done, cool and set aside. Preheat a large non-stick sauté pan over medium-high heat. Add garlic, onions, bell peppers to skillet and cook, stirring occasionally until vegetables are softened and lightly caramelized. Cool and reserve. Combine all vegetables once cooled and add oil and vinegar. Stir in thyme, salt and pepper to taste. Top with green onions and serve cold.

Serving size: 1/2 cup

Yields: 8 servings

Nutrition Facts (per serving): 85 calories, 1g total fat, 0g saturated fat, 42mg sodium, 18g carbohydrates, 3g fiber, *Gluten-Free*

Healthy Living Tip

Sweet potatoes provide fiber, vitamin A, vitamin C, and potassium. Sweet potatoes also have a lower glycemic index value than white potatoes. This makes a colorful tailgate party recipe.

Whole Wheat Pasta Salad

13 ounces dry whole wheat pasta

12 ounces roasted red peppers

1 ½ cups broccoli florets

1/2 cup reduced-fat feta cheese

1 tablespoon olive oil

1 cup Maple Grove Farms Fat-Free Balsamic Vinaigrette

4 tablespoons fresh basil, chiffonade

Cook pasta according to directions on the box, chill and reserve. Blanch the broccoli for 2-3 minutes in boiling water and transfer to an ice water bath to chill. Broccoli should still be firm but not crunchy. Drain juice from the peppers, remove any seeds and ribs, and cut into 1/4-inch by 1-inch strips. Cut the broccoli into florets. Chiffonade basil. In a large bowl, combine all the ingredients and allow to marinate for at least 2 hours.

Serving size: 1/2 cup

Yields: 20 servings

Nutrition Facts (per serving): 180 calories, 6g total fat, 2g saturated fat, 270mg sodium, 33g carbohydrates, 5g fiber.

Vegetables and Fruits

*Featured: Sautéed Asparagus with Roasted Red Pepper and
Summer Squash with Cherry Tomatoes and Basil*

Baked Apple Compote

2 cinnamon sticks, each broken into 3 pieces

6 whole cloves

3 golden delicious apples (about 18 ounces), halved, cored

1 teaspoon fresh lemon juice

Preheat oven to 325F degrees. Insert 1 piece of cinnamon stick and 1 clove into each half of an apple. Arrange apples, cut side down, on a baking sheet and bake for about 30 minutes until the apples are soft. Cool slightly and remove and discard cinnamon sticks and cloves. Scoop flesh from apples into a medium bowl and add the lemon juice. Using a fork, coarsely mash the apples. Season the compote with salt and freshly ground pepper. Serve warm.

Serving size: 1/2 cup

Yields: 4 servings

Nutrition Facts (per serving): 61 calories, 0g total fat, 0g saturated fat, 0mg sodium, 16g carbohydrates, 2g fiber, *Gluten-Free*

Healthy Living Tip

This recipe can be used as a topping for the Diet Dr. Pepper Pork Loin recipe.

Balsamic-Marinated Asparagus

1 pound fresh asparagus spears

1 tablespoon balsamic vinegar

1 tablespoon olive oil

1/2 teaspoon lemon zest

1/4 teaspoon salt

1/4 teaspoon pepper

Cut off the ends of the asparagus. Blanch the asparagus by cooking in boiling water for 2-3 minutes, depending on size. Remove from heat and place in a bowl with ice water to stop the cooking process. Marinate the asparagus in oil and vinegar for 20 minutes, then add them to a sauté pan on medium heat with olive oil, salt, pepper and lemon zest. Cook for about 3 minutes or until the vegetables are slightly tender.

Serving size: 1/2 cup

Yields: 4 servings

Nutrition Facts (per serving): 30 calories, 2g total fat, 0g saturated fat, 40mg sodium, 5g carbohydrates, 2g fiber, *Gluten-Free*

Healthy Living Tip

This is a low-fat, high fiber recipe that adds flavor to any meal. Asparagus is an anti-inflammatory food that helps your body fight inflammatory diseases like heart disease, diabetes, and arthritis.

Broccoli Casserole

20 ounces fresh broccoli florets

10 ounces reduced-sodium cream of mushroom soup

1/2 cup fat-free mayonnaise

1/4 cup evaporated skim milk

1/4 cup shredded, low-fat cheddar cheese

2 egg whites, slightly beaten

1/4 cup Panko bread crumbs

1 tablespoon trans-fat free margarine, melted

non-stick cooking spray

Preheat oven to 350F degrees. Coat a 9 x 9-inch pan with cooking spray. Lay the broccoli evenly in pan. In a medium bowl, combine the soup, mayonnaise, evaporated milk, cheese and egg whites, then mix well and pour over the broccoli. In a small bowl using a fork, combine the bread crumbs with margarine until they are thoroughly mixed, then sprinkle over the soup and broccoli mixture. Bake 40 to 45 minutes or until golden.

Serving size: 1/6 recipe

Yields: 6 servings

Nutrition Facts (per serving): 118 calories, 3g total fat, <1g saturated fat, 400mg sodium, 18g carbohydrates, 3.5g fiber.

Healthy Living Tip

Broccoli, cauliflower and Brussels sprouts are cruciferous vegetables. Cruciferous vegetables are well known for their cancer prevention properties.

Broccoli Layer Salad with Dried Cranberries

8 cups broccoli florets, cut into small pieces

1 cup red onion, sliced

1/3 cup dried cranberries

1/3 cup reduced-fat sharp cheddar cheese, shredded

1/2 cup plain Greek yogurt

2 tablespoons cider vinegar

1 1/2 tablespoons agave nectar

1 tablespoon canola oil mayonnaise

2 tablespoons pumpkin seeds, roasted

In a large glass trifle or serving bowl, layer the broccoli, onion, cranberries and cheese. In a small bowl, whisk the yogurt, vinegar, agave nectar and mayonnaise. Pour the dressing evenly over the salad. Garnish with the pumpkin seeds.

Serving size: 1/6 recipe

Yields: 6 servings

Nutrition Facts (per serving): 130 calories, 5g total fat, 1g saturated fat, 95mg sodium, 18g carbohydrates, 3g fiber, *Gluten-Free*

Healthy Living Tip

The yogurt-based dressing has less fat and fewer calories than mayonnaise. A small portion of pumpkin seeds add healthy fats and fiber which can improve your blood cholesterol levels.

Broccoli with Orange and Basil

2 cups broccoli florets

2 oranges, segmented or canned Mandarin oranges

1/4 cup fresh basil chiffonade

1 1/2 teaspoons orange zest

Steam the broccoli and oranges for about 3 minutes until the broccoli is bright green and tender crisp. Add the zest and basil, then toss. Divide among 4 plates and serve.

Serving size: 1/2 cup

Yields: 4 servings

Nutrition Facts (per serving): 54 calories, 0g total fat, 0g saturated fat, 10mg sodium, 13g carbohydrates, 2g fiber, *Gluten-Free*

Healthy Living Tip

This is a great recipe to serve as a cold salad as well. Just blanch and shock the broccoli before mixing the other ingredients.

To segment the orange, cut off both ends and rest it on one of the flat ends. Starting at the top of the fruit and using the middle of the knife blade, cut away the skin and pith. Slice each segment away from the connective membrane and use the knife to scoop the segments out.

Collard Greens with Smoked Turkey

3 pounds fresh collard greens, trimmed and washed

4 ounces smoked turkey breasts, cubed (or use cubed cooked fresh turkey)

2 cups red onions, finely chopped

2 tablespoons canola oil

2 1/2 cups vegetable broth, reduced sodium

1/4 cup cider vinegar

1 1/2 tablespoons brown sugar

1/2 tablespoon dried, crushed red pepper

1 1/2 teaspoons salt substitute

In a heavy bottom stock pot, add oil and sauté the turkey until it's slightly caramelized. Add the onions and sauté until tender. Next, add the broth, vinegar, brown sugar, and spices. Gradually add the collards to a Dutch oven and cook, stirring occasionally, 8 to 10 minutes or just until they're wilted. Reduce the heat to medium and cook 1 hour or until tender, stirring occasionally.

Serving size: 1/8 recipe

Yields: 8 servings

Nutrition Facts (per serving): 105 calories, 4g total fat, 1g saturated fat, 329mg sodium, 15g carbohydrates, 7g fiber, **_Gluten-Free_**

Healthy Living Tip

Reduce the preparation time by using washed and trimmed collard greens available in most produce sections. Collard greens are rich sources of vitamin K. Collard greens have the ability to reduce blood cholesterol levels and offer cancer prevention properties.

Cranberry-Apple Relish

12 ounces fresh cranberries

1 cup Splenda

1 cup orange juice

1 medium Fuji apple, peeled, cored, and diced

1/3 cup golden raisins

Place the cranberries, Splenda, and orange juice in a medium saucepan and bring to a boil. Boil for 3-4 minutes or until the cranberries start to thicken and the water has reduced to about half. Remove from the pan and place into a medium bowl. Cover and refrigerate 2-3 hours or overnight. Add diced apple and raisins to the cranberry mixture and stir well. Refrigerate until ready to serve.

Serving size: 2 tablespoons

Yields: 20 servings

Nutrition Facts (per serving): 25 calories, 0g total fat, 0g saturated fat, 2mg sodium, 6g carbohydrates, 1g fiber, *Gluten-Free*

Healthy Living Tip

This is great as a side dish or condiment for beef, turkey, and chicken. Fresh cranberry relish has more fiber and much less sugar than canned cranberry sauce.

Crunchy Kickoff Coleslaw

1/4 cup lime juice

1/4 cup rice vinegar

3 tablespoons poblano pepper

2 teaspoons agave nectar

1 1/2 tablespoons olive oil

1 teaspoon lime zest

1/2 teaspoon sea salt

6 cups cabbage, thinly sliced

2 cups jicama, peeled and grated

1 cup carrot, peeled and grated

3/4 cup green onion, thinly sliced

1/4 cup chopped fresh cilantro

1/4 cup chopped fresh mint

Combine the lime juice, vinegar, chopped pepper, agave nectar, olive oil, lime zest, and salt in a small bowl, stirring with a whisk. In a large bowl add the cabbage and the remaining ingredients. Pour the dressing over the cabbage mixture tossing gently to coat. Serve immediately.

Serving size: 1 cup

Yields: 8 cups

Nutrition Facts (per serving): 65 calories, 3g total fat, 0g saturated fat, 144mg sodium, 12g carbohydrates, 3g fiber, *Gluten-Free*

Healthy Living Tip

To lighten any coleslaw dish use fresh herbs, onion, garlic, fruit juices, and flavored vinegars.

Fresh Corn Salsa

1 1/2 teaspoons olive oil

1 cup corn, fresh cut

1/4 teaspoon sugar

1 tablespoon balsamic vinegar

2 chopped, fresh plum tomatoes

1/4 cup red onion, chopped

1/4 cup chopped cilantro leaves

1 jalapeno, diced

salt and pepper to taste

In large sauté pan, add the oil and heat on medium heat. Add the corn and cook for 2 minutes. Add the sugar, season with salt and pepper, and cook for another minute. Add vinegar and cook for another minute. Transfer the corn into a bowl and cool slightly. Stir in the tomatoes, onion, cilantro and jalapeno pepper. Serve as a side dish or as a topping for chicken.

Serving size: 1/4 cup

Yields: 4 servings

Nutrition Facts (per serving): 60 calories, 2g total fat, 0g saturated fat, 75mg sodium, 10g carbohydrates, 1g fiber, *Gluten-Free*

Fresh Green Bean Sauté

12 ounces fresh green beans, trimmed

2 ounces tomatoes

2 tablespoons fresh basil

1 tablespoon olive oil

sea salt to taste

Blanch the green beans in boiling water for 3-4 minutes or until they're lightly cooked but still a vibrant green. In a medium sauté pan heat the olive oil, then add the green beans and sauté for 30 seconds. Next add tomatoes and basil and cook for 30 seconds more. Add salt to taste.

Serving size: 1/2 cup

Yields: 4 servings

Nutrition Facts (per serving): 45 calories, 1g total fat, 0g saturated fat, 50mg sodium, 5g carbohydrates, 3g fiber, *Gluten-Free*

Mixed Bean and Sun-Dried Tomato Salad

1 15-ounce can green beans, drained

1 15-ounce can yellow wax beans, drained

1 15-ounce can kidney beans, drained

1 15-ounce can garbanzo beans, rinsed and drained

4 ounces sun-dried tomatoes, softened and minced

1/4 cup onion, chopped

1/4 cup basil, chiffonade

1/4 cup orange juice

1/2 cup balsamic vinegar

Combine the beans, sun-dried tomatoes, onions and basil in a mixing bowl, then add vinegar and orange juice. Allow to sit for 3 minutes before serving.

Serving size: 1/2 cup

Yields: 14 servings

Nutrition Facts (per serving): 103 calories, <1g total fat, <1g saturated fat, 343mg sodium, 20g carbohydrates, 5g fiber, *Gluten-Free*

Healthy Living Tip

This simple, colorful bean salad is a great source of fiber and protein, a healthy addition to any meal.

Sautéed Asparagus with Roasted Red Peppers

1 pound fresh asparagus spears	1/4 teaspoon pepper
1 red bell pepper	1/4 teaspoon dried basil
1 tablespoon olive oil	1/4 teaspoon dried oregano
1/8 teaspoon salt	1/4 teaspoon dried thyme leaves

To roast the pepper: Place red pepper in a preheated oven set on broil and cook for 15-20 minutes or until charred. Place the pepper in zip-top bag and let it sweat for about 10 minutes. Take the pepper out and remove the skin and seeds, then slice.

To blanch the asparagus: Cut off the ends of the asparagus. Blanch the asparagus by cooking it in boiling water for 3 minutes. Remove from heat and place in a bowl with ice water to stop the cooking process. Combine the roasted red pepper and asparagus in a sauté pan on medium heat with olive oil, salt, pepper and spices. Cook for about 5 minutes or until the vegetables are slightly tender.

Serving size: 1/2 cup

Yields: 4 servings

Nutrition Facts (per serving): 30 calories, 30g total fat, 0g saturated fat, 40mg sodium, 5g carbohydrates, 8.5g fiber, *Gluten-Free*

Healthy Living Tip

Roasted red peppers freeze well. Roast extra peppers when making this recipe to freeze so they are available during the winter when the cost of peppers is higher.

Spiced Apples

2 1/4 cups fresh apples, peeled and diced

1/4 cup Splenda

1 1/2 tablespoons water

1 1/2 teaspoons lemon juice

1/2 cup raisins

3/4 teaspoon cinnamon

Place apples in a saucepan, then add Splenda, water, lemon juice, raisins and cinnamon. Stir well to blend. Cook over medium heat, stirring occasionally, until the mixture begins to thicken. Cook until the apples are tender. Portion 1/2 cup apple mixture in each serving dish and garnish with a sprinkle of cinnamon. Serve warm.

Serving Size: 1/2 cup

Yields: 4 servings

Nutrition Facts (per serving): 60 calories, 0g total fat, 0g saturated fat, 3mg sodium, 16g carbohydrates, 2g fiber, *Gluten-Free*

Stuffed Acorn Squash

3 small acorn squash (4 inches in diameter)

1 cup cooked brown rice

1 cup 3/4-inch cubed baguette or your favorite artisan bread

1 cup medium onion, chopped

1/2 cup fat-free, low-sodium chicken broth

1/4 cup dried cranberries

2 tablespoons chopped walnuts, toasted

1 tablespoon butter, whipped

1/2 teaspoon sage, fresh chopped

1/4 teaspoon oregano, fresh chopped

1/4 teaspoon salt

1/4 teaspoon pepper

1/4 cup water

Preheat oven to 400F degrees. Cut each squash in half and scoop and discard the seeds and strings. In a large bowl, mix the remaining ingredients. Fill the squash halves loosely with the stuffing mixture. Pour the water into a 13 x 9-inch casserole dish. Place the squash halves with the filled side up in the dish. Cover and bake for 60 to 75 minutes or until the squash is tender when pierced with the tip of a knife.

Serving size: 1 filled acorn squash

Yields: 6 servings

Nutrition Facts (per serving): 193 calories, 3g total fat, <1g saturated fat, 158mg sodium, 40g carbohydrates, 5g fiber.

Summer Squash with Cherry Tomatoes and Basil

1 tablespoon olive oil

1 pound yellow squash, sliced

8 cherry tomatoes, halved

1 tablespoon basil, chopped

salt and pepper to taste

Heat oil in a sauté pan over medium heat, then add the squash and sauté until lightly caramelized. Add tomatoes and basil, then toss to heat. Season with salt and pepper.

Serving size: 1/2 cup

Yields: 4 servings

Nutrition Facts (per serving): 44 calories, 3g total fat, 0g saturated fat, 11mg sodium, 4g carbohydrates, 1.5g fiber, *Gluten-Free*

Healthy Living Tip

This recipe incorporates well into the Mediterranean diet because of the fresh vegetables, herbs, and olive oil.

Swiss Chard and Onion

1/2 teaspoon garlic

8 cups Swiss chard, raw chopped

2 1/2 cups sweet yellow onion, julienne

2 tablespoons white wine

1/2 tablespoon garlic

salt and pepper to taste

Heat a sauté pan over medium-high heat. Add olive oil and garlic, then sauté about 15 seconds until the garlic is lightly browned. Add the onions and cook until translucent, then add the chard and sauté for another minute or until it's lightly wilted. Deglaze with wine and season with salt and pepper.

Serving size: 1/2 cup

Yields: 4 servings

Nutrition Facts (per serving): 13 calories, 2g total fat, 0g saturated fat, 209mg sodium, 26g carbohydrates, 4g fiber, *Gluten-Free*

Healthy Living Tip

Swiss chard is considered one of the world's healthiest vegetables. It provides many phytonutrient antioxidant sources from the rich dark green in its leaves and vibrant pink, purple, and orange in its stalks.

Desserts

Featured: Grilled Peaches with Cinnamon, Walnuts and Basil, Dark Chocolate Covered Fruit and Strawberry Parfaits

Banana Bread Muffins

2 cups almond flour

1/2 teaspoon sea salt

1/2 teaspoon baking soda

1 teaspoon ground cinnamon

1/4 cup canola oil

1/2 cup agave nectar

2 omega-3 eggs

1 1/2 cups ripe banana, mashed

1/2 cup walnuts, coarsely chopped

1 teaspoon vanilla extract

Preheat oven to 350F degrees. Grease muffin pans with canola oil and dust with almond flour. In a large bowl, combine almond flour, salt, baking soda, and cinnamon. In a medium bowl, whisk the canola oil, agave nectar, vanilla, and eggs together. Blend the almond flour mixture into the wet ingredients until they are thoroughly combined, then fold in the bananas and walnuts. Scoop the batter into the muffin pans until 2/3 full and bake for 25 minutes on the bottom rack of the oven, until a knife inserted into the center of a muffin comes out clean. Let the bread cool in the pans for 10 minutes and turn out onto a wire rack.

Serving size: 1 muffin

Yields: 16 muffins

Nutrition Facts (per serving): 194 calories, 14g total fat, 1.5g saturated fat, 118mg sodium, 17g carbohydrates, 2.5g fiber, *Gluten-Free*

Healthy Living Tip

Almond flour, like all nuts, is high in monounsaturated fat and low in carbohydrates. Store almond flour in the freezer to extend its shelf-life. These muffins are great to freeze for a quick and healthy breakfast. To thaw, simply remove from freezer and allow muffin to return to room temperature, about 10 minutes.

Banana Delight

1 tablespoon whipped butter or trans-free margarine

1 tablespoon walnut oil

1 tablespoon agave nectar

2 tablespoons firmly packed brown sugar

1/2 teaspoon cinnamon

3 tablespoons skim milk

4 firm bananas (approx. 1 pound)

1/2 teaspoon canola oil

2 tablespoons dark rum or apple juice

light whipped topping

In a small saucepan, melt the butter over medium heat. Whisk in the oil, agave, brown sugar, and cinnamon, then cook for about 3 minutes, stirring constantly until the sugar is dissolved. Stir in the milk, 1 tablespoon at a time, then cook for about 3 minutes, stirring constantly until the sauce thickens slightly. Remove from heat, set aside. Peel the bananas and cut each one crosswise into 3 sections. Cut each section in half lengthwise. Lightly coat a large, non-stick frying pan with canola oil and place over medium-high heat. Add the bananas and sauté until they begin to brown, 3-4 minutes. Transfer to a plate. Add the rum or juice to the pan, bring to boil and deglaze the pan. Cook for 30-45 seconds until it's reduced by half. Return the bananas to the pan to re-warm. To serve, divide the bananas among serving plates. Drizzle with warm sauce and top each with 2 tablespoons of light whipped topping.

Serving size: 1/6 recipe

Yields: 6 servings

Nutrition Facts (per serving): 156 calories, 5g total fat, 2g saturated fat, 25mg sodium, 28g carbohydrates, 2g fiber, *Gluten-Free*

Healthy Living Tip

Cinnamon has the highest antioxidant capacity of any spice.

Bittersweet Chocolate Meringues

1/8 teaspoon salt

1/8 teaspoon cream of tartar

3 egg whites

1/2 cup sugar

1/4 cup finely chopped bittersweet chocolate

Preheat oven to 225F degrees. Line two baking sheets with parchment paper and set aside. Place the salt, cream of tartar and egg whites in a large bowl and beat with a mixer at high speed until foamy. Add sugar, 1 tablespoon at a time, beating until stiff peaks form. Beat for 1 minute at high speed or until the mixture is shiny. Gently fold in the chocolate. Spoon the mixture into a large zip-top plastic bag. Snip a 1/4-inch hole in one bottom corner of the bag. Pipe 24 (4-inch-long) zigzag shapes onto each prepared pan. Bake for 30 minutes with one pan on the bottom rack and one pan on the second rack from top. Rotate the pans and bake an additional 30 minutes or until dry to the touch. Cool on pans for 30 minutes on wire racks. Carefully remove meringues from paper and let cool completely on wire racks. You can store meringues in an airtight container at room temperature for up to two weeks.

Serving size: 2 cookies

Yields: 12 servings

Nutrition Facts (per serving): 54 calories, 1g total fat, <1g saturated fat, 39mg sodium, 11g carbohydrates, <1g fiber, *Gluten-Free*

Healthy Living Tip

Bittersweet chocolate is also referred to as dark chocolate. Dark chocolate contains flavonoids. Flavonoids are antioxidants that can fight free radicals to help prevent cancer and heart disease. Look for dark chocolate containing at least 70% cocoa.

Cannoli Tartlets

1 15-ounce carton part-skim ricotta cheese

1/4 cup Splenda

4 ounces mini chocolate chips

pinch of ground cinnamon

1 teaspoon vanilla extract

1 tablespoon cocoa powder (optional)

30 frozen mini phyllo shells

canned fat-free whipped topping

In a medium bowl, stir ricotta, sugar substitute, chocolate chips, cinnamon, vanilla, and cocoa powder together until well combined, cover and chill. No more than 2 hours before serving, fill the mini phyllo shells with about 1 tablespoon of ricotta filling and refrigerate until ready to serve. Add whipped topping just before serving. The ricotta filling can be made up to 1 day in advance and refrigerated in a covered container. Tartlets can be filled up to 2 hours ahead of time and refrigerated, lightly covered until ready to serve.

Serving size: 1 tartlet

Yields: 30 tartlets

Nutrition Facts (per serving): 70 calories, 3g total fat, 1g saturated fat, 30mg sodium, 5g carbohydrates, 0g fiber.

Healthy Living Tip

Guilt-free Chocolate Options	CALORIES	FAT (GRAMS)
Dark Chocolate, 1 oz.	150	5
Hot Chocolate (No Sugar Added)	50	0
Chocolate Teddy Grahams (24 pieces)	150	5
Light chocolate pudding 1 cup	100	0
Chocolate Meringue Cookie	25	0
Chocolate Covered Strawberry	45	2
Sugar-free Fudgsicle	40	1
Oreo 100 Calorie Pack	100	1
Sugar Free Chocolate Syrup 2T.	15	0

Chef Walter's Easy Fruit Salad

1 bag frozen mixed fruit

1 bag frozen pineapple chunks

8 ounces fat-free, no-added-sugar yogurt (flavor of choice)

Thaw fruit at room temperature. Toss with yogurt. Serve immediately.

Serving Size: ½ cup

Yields: 8 servings

Nutrition Facts (per serving): 75 calories, 0g total fat, 0g saturated fat, 8mg sodium, 17g carbohydrates, 2g fiber, *Gluten-Free*

Chef Walter's Guilt Free Cheesecake

1/2 cup vanilla wafer or chocolate cookie crumbs

2 8-ounce packages 1/3 less fat cream cheese (not fat-free)

2/3 cup Splenda

3/4 cup egg substitute (like Egg Beaters or Great Eggs-pectations)

2 teaspoons vanilla extract

2 teaspoons lemon extract

2 cups low-fat vanilla yogurt

2 tablespoons all-purpose flour

Preheat oven to 300F degrees. Spray a 9 or 10-inch spring-form pan with cooking oil spray and sprinkle the crumbs evenly over the bottom. Beat the cream cheese with an electric mixer until smooth. Add the Splenda, eggs, vanilla, and lemon extract and beat on medium speed about 2 minutes or until well blended and smooth. Scrape down sides of the bowl, if necessary. Add yogurt and flour and continue to beat until smooth. Carefully spread the batter over the crumbs, then bake for 1 hour. Turn off the oven and allow to stand 30 minutes. Remove from oven and cool another 30 minutes. Cover and refrigerate at least 3 or 4 hours. You can serve this plain or pour warm, sugar free jam over the top.

Serving size: 1 slice or 1/10 recipe

Yields: 10 servings

Nutrition Facts (per serving): 177 calories, 9g total fat, 5g saturated fat, 289mg sodium, 16g carbohydrates, 0g fiber.

Healthy Living Tip

One slice of regular cheesecake can take up at least half of your daily needs for saturated fat. Restaurant mega-portions can contain double your amount of saturated fat per day. Try this low-fat cheesecake for a healthier treat.

Chef Walter's Low-Fat Brownies

1 package brownie mix, 13 x 9-inch pan size

1 egg

1/2 cup prune puree (or applesauce)

1/2 cup water

Blend all ingredients and turn into a greased 13 x 9-inch pan. Bake according to the package directions.

Serving size: 1 brownie

Yields: 20 servings

Nutrition Facts (per serving): 126 calories, 2g total fat, 0g saturated fat, 152mg sodium, 27g carbohydrates, 1g fiber.

Healthy Living Tip

This recipe is 50 calories less than a typical brownie serving. To reduce the fat in other baked goods recipes, substitute at least half the fat (oil, margarine or butter) content with applesauce, mashed bananas or prune puree.

To make prune puree: place 9 pitted medium prunes and 1/3 cup of boiling water in a food processor. Process the mixture until smooth. Cool to room temperature before using.

Chocolate Banana Bread

1 cup all-purpose flour

1 cup whole wheat flour

3/4 teaspoon baking soda

1/2 teaspoon salt substitute

1/2 cup sugar

1/4 cup trans-free margarine

1 1/2 cups banana, mashed

1/2 cup egg substitute

1/3 cup plain nonfat yogurt

1/2 cup semi-sweet chocolate chips

non-stick cooking spray

Preheat oven to 350F degrees. Lightly spoon flours into dry measuring cups and level with a knife. Combine the flours, baking soda, and salt substitute, stirring with a whisk. Place sugar and margarine in separate bowl and beat at medium speed for about 1 minute until well blended. Add the banana, egg substitute and yogurt, then beat until blended. Add the flour mixture and beat at low speed, just until moist. Place the chocolate chips in a medium bowl and microwave for 1 minute or until almost melted, stirring until smooth. Cool slightly, then add 1 cup of batter to the chocolate, stirring until well combined. Spoon the chocolate batter alternately with plain batter into an 8 1/2 x 4 1/2-inch loaf pan coated with cooking spray. Swirl the batters together with a knife to give a marbled effect. Bake for 75 minutes or until a wooden toothpick inserted in the center comes out clean. Cool for 10 minutes in a pan on a wire rack, then remove from pan. Cool completely on a wire rack.

Serving size: 1/16 recipe

Yields: 16 servings

Nutrition Facts (per serving): 140 calories, 4g total fat, 1g saturated fat, 100mg sodium, 26g carbohydrates, 1g fiber.

Healthy Living Tip

To increase the fiber in baked goods, cut the amount of white flour in half and replace it with whole wheat flour.

Chocolate Walnut Mousse Phyllo Cup with Fresh Fruit

6 phyllo sheets

butter flavored cooking spray

2 cups skim milk

1 small box sugar-free, instant chocolate pudding

1 cup fat-free sour cream

1 8-ounce container frozen, fat-free whipped topping, thawed

4 ounces toasted crushed walnuts

3 cups strawberries, diced

½ cup orange juice

4 teaspoons Splenda

Preheat oven to 375F degrees. Cover stack of phyllo sheets with 2 overlapping layers of plastic wrap and a dampened kitchen towel. Put 1 phyllo sheet on a work surface and spray with cooking spray, then top with 2 more sheets of phyllo, spraying each with cooking spray. Cut stack into 6 (4 1/2-inch) squares with a sharp knife, trimming sides as needed. Line 6 muffin cups with a 4 ½-inch square stack. Repeat process to make 6 more phyllo cups. Bake cups in middle of oven until golden, about 8 minutes, then cool completely in pan on a rack.

Pour milk into a large bowl, then add the pudding whisking together for 1 full minute or until smooth and creamy. Add the sour cream and whipped topping and whisk until smooth. Cover and refrigerate for at least 3 hours to set. Mix together strawberries, orange juice and Splenda, then allow to rest for 30 minutes, refrigerated. Scoop the mousse into phyllo cups and top with toasted walnuts. Drizzle fruit around the cup on a plate with some of the juices.

Serving size: one prepared phyllo cup

Yields: 12 servings

Nutrition Facts (per serving): 169 calories, 9g total fat, 2.8g saturated fat, 222mg sodium, 19g carbohydrates, 2g fiber.

Healthy Living Tip

How to toast walnuts: Preheat oven to 375F degrees. Lay walnuts on baking sheet. Roast walnuts until they start to brown and smell toasted, 5-10 minutes. Walnuts are a heart-healthy food choice, because they are a source of omega-3 fatty acids.

Coconut Macaroons

4 egg whites

1/4 teaspoon salt

1 teaspoon vanilla

2 cups shredded unsweetened coconut

1/4 cup agave nectar

1 tablespoon cocoa powder (optional)

Preheat oven to 350F degrees. Line a baking sheet with parchment paper and then set aside. Add egg whites and salt to a mixer and beat until stiff peaks form. Fold in vanilla, agave nectar, coconut, and cocoa powder (optional). Drop by rounded tablespoon on a lined baking sheet. Shape with a cookie cutter if desired. For basket shaped cookies, roll into a ball and indent the center before baking. Bake approximately 15 minutes or until golden brown. Transfer to a wire rack with a spatula to cool. To serve, fill basket shaped cookies with sugar-free jellybeans.

Serving size: 1 cookie

Yields: 18 cookies

Nutrition Facts (per serving): 68 calories, 6g total fat, 5g saturated fat, 48mg sodium, 4g carbohydrates, 2g fiber, *Gluten-Free*

Healthy Living Tip

Although coconut is high in saturated fat, it is a good variety of saturated fat due to the higher amounts of medium chain fatty acids (MCFA). MCFAs are used to produce energy in the body and not to produce body fat. Eat fresh coconut and its counterparts, coconut oil and milk, in moderation much like oils and nuts.

Dark Chocolate Brownies

1/3 cup butter

2/3 cup agave syrup

1 ounce unsweetened chocolate (we like Ghiradelli)

2 large eggs

1 teaspoon vanilla extract

1/2 cup quinoa flour

1/2 cup unsweetened cocoa

1/4 teaspoon baking powder

1/4 teaspoon salt

1/4 cup sliced almonds

1 teaspoon espresso granules

Glaze

2-3 Mandarin orange segments

¼ cup powdered sugar

Preheat oven to 325F degrees. Grease mini-muffin pans (makes 24 mini muffins). In a medium saucepan melt the butter over low heat. Add the chocolate and stir just until melted, then remove from heat. Stir in the agave syrup with a wooden spoon. Stir in the eggs, 1 at a time, until well blended. Add vanilla and espresso. In a medium bowl, combine flour, cocoa, baking powder, and salt. Stir flour mixture into saucepan until blended. Stir in the almonds, then spoon the batter into the mini-muffin pans. Bake 10-14 minutes until a toothpick comes out clean.

To prepare glaze, mash Mandarin oranges with a fork and add powdered sugar to a thin icing consistency. Top brownie with a 1/2 teaspoon of glaze.

Serving size: 1 brownie

Yields: 24 servings

Nutrition Facts (per serving): 110 calories, 5g total fat, 3g saturated fat, 40mg sodium, 14g carbohydrates, 1g fiber, *Gluten-Free*

Dark Chocolate Covered Fruit

6 ounces dark chocolate

3 tablespoons fat-free half and half

20 orange slices, strawberries, grapes (fruit of choice)

Heat the chocolate in a glass bowl in a microwave oven on high for 1 minute. Stir, then heat at additional 15 second intervals until the chocolate is melted. Add half and half, and whisk together. Dip each piece of fruit into the chocolate mixture allowing the excess chocolate to drip back into the bowl. If necessary, add additional cream to the chocolate to achieve the desired coating consistency. Transfer the coated fruit to a baking sheet lined with waxed paper. Allow the chocolate coated fruit to cool and chill until the chocolate is set, about 20 to 30 minutes.

Serving size: 2 pieces dipped fruit

Yields: 10 servings

Nutrition Facts (per serving): 45 calories, 2g total fat, 1g saturated fat, 14mg sodium, 7g carbohydrates, 1g fiber, *Gluten-Free*

Healthy Living Tip

Fruits and nuts enhance the nutritional value of chocolate by adding fiber, antioxidants, and healthy monounsaturated fats. Research shows that antioxidants and flavonoids in dark chocolate may help prevent cholesterol from sticking to artery walls, reducing your risk of heart attack or stroke.

Dream Berry Cheesecake

Crust

1/3 cup ground flaxseed

1/2 cup ground pecans

1/2 cup graham cracker crumbs

2 tablespoons trans-free margarine

Filling

3 8-ounce packages 1/3 less fat cream cheese

1 8-ounce package fat-free cream cheese

1/2 cup sugar

1 12-ounce package frozen mixed berries, thawed and drained

1 8-ounce container frozen, light whipped topping, thawed and divided

Crust: In a food processor, combine the flaxseed, pecans, graham cracker crumbs and blend to crumb consistency. Melt the margarine and pour over the mixture. Press into a 13 x 9-inch dish. Bake in the oven at 350F degrees for 10-12 minutes or until lightly browned. Cool before adding the filling.

Filling: Beat cream cheese and sugar with an electric mixer on medium speed until well blended. Smash the drained berries with a fork and stir into the cheese mixture. Gently stir in 2 cups of whipped topping. Spoon the mixture over the crust. Cover and refrigerate for 4 hours or until firm. Top with remaining whipped topping.

Serving size: 1/20 recipe

Yields: 20 servings

Nutrition Facts (per serving): 200 calories, 12g total fat, 5g saturated fat, 165mg sodium, 12g carbohydrates, 1g fiber.

Healthy Living Tip

The crust in this recipe uses flaxseed and pecans instead of butter giving it a richer taste with less saturated fat. Eating 1-2 tablespoons of ground flaxseed per day can improve blood cholesterol levels.

Grilled Peaches with Cinnamon, Walnuts and Basil

2 peaches, halved

1/2 teaspoon cinnamon

1 tablespoon Splenda Brown Sugar Blend

4 ounces non-fat vanilla yogurt

2 ounces toasted walnuts

2 tablespoons fresh basil, chiffonade

Preheat oven to 350F degrees. Sear peaches on medium-high heat directly on a grill or on stovetop in a non-stick sauté pan. In a small bowl, mix the cinnamon and sugar together and sprinkle on top of the peaches. Transfer peaches to a baking sheet and place in oven to prevent burning. Bake for 15 minutes or until soft on the outside. Place each peach on a plate, and top with yogurt. Garnish with walnuts and basil.

Serving size: 1/4 recipe

Yields: 4 servings

Nutrition Facts (per serving): 144 calories, 9g total fat, 2g saturated fat, 2mg sodium, 14g carbohydrates, 2g fiber, *Gluten-Free*

Healthy Living Tip

This recipe is a great component of the Mediterranean diet because of the simple use of fruit and little sugar or fat. Nutritionally peaches are great sources of vitamin C and E as well as folate and niacin.

Key Lime Treats

1 14-ounce can fat-free, sweetened condensed milk

1/2 teaspoon lime zest

1/2 cup Key Lime juice

1 drop green and yellow food coloring each (optional)

24 frozen mini phyllo shells

canned fat-free whipped topping

thin lime wedges, quartered (optional)

In a small bowl, gradually whisk sweetened condensed milk, lime zest, lime juice, and food coloring, if desired, together. Cover and chill for about 2 hours or until the mixture mounds slightly. Spoon about 1 tablespoon of filling into each phyllo shell right before serving. Top with whipped topping and quartered lime wedges.

Serving size: 1 tart

Yields: 24 tarts

Nutrition Facts (per serving): 57 calories, 1g total fat, 0g saturated fat, 10mg sodium, 8g carbohydrates, 0g fiber.

Healthy Living Tip

This is a great dessert for portion control. You can eat 2 tarts and stay on track for daily calorie and carbohydrate consumption. This recipe does not leave you deprived of a dessert.

Lemon Blueberry Cake

1 tablespoon all-purpose flour

1 8 ounce package yellow cake mix

1 teaspoon almond extract

3 large egg whites

1 large omega-3 egg

8 ounce fat-free cream cheese, softened

1/3 cup fresh lemon juice

1 cup fresh blueberries

2 tablespoons flour

non-stick cooking spray

For Glaze

1 tablespoon lemon juice, freshly squeezed

1/2 cup powdered sugar

Preheat oven to 350F degrees. Coat a 12-cup Bundt pan with cooking spray and dust with flour. Combine the cake mix, almond extract, egg whites, omega-3 egg, cream cheese and lemon juice in a large bowl and beat with an electric mixer on low for 30 seconds. Then beat on medium speed for 2 minutes. Coat the blueberries with 1 tablespoon of flour and fold into batter. Pour batter into the prepared pan. Bake for 50 minutes or until a wooden toothpick inserted in the center comes out clean. Cool the cake for 10 minutes, then remove from the pan and cool completely on a wire rack. Combine the powdered sugar and lemon juice in a small bowl and drizzle over the cake.

Serving size: 1 slice (1/18 cake)

Yields: 18 servings

Nutrition Facts (per serving): 182 calories, 4g total fat, 1g saturated fat, 300mg sodium, 32g carbohydrates, 1g fiber.

Healthy Living Tip

Coating the blueberries with flour prevents the blueberries from settling in the bottom of the pan. Making modifications in this recipe saves 160 calories, 9 grams of fat, and 20 grams of carbohydrate.

Light Pumpkin Pudding

2 cups canned pumpkin

1/4 cup Splenda Sugar Blend

1 teaspoon maple extract

2 tablespoon maple syrup

1/2 cup reduced-fat sour cream

1/2 cup evaporated skim milk

1 large egg beaten

2 large egg whites

1 1/2 teaspoons cinnamon

1 teaspoon lemon zest

1/2 teaspoon ground ginger

1/2 teaspoon ground cloves

pinch of salt

light whipped topping

non-stick cooking spray

Preheat oven to 375F degrees. Spray 6 (8-ounce) ramekins with cooking spray. Combine all of the ingredients, *except the evaporated skim milk*, in a food processor or mixer and puree or beat until smooth. Slowly pour in the evaporated skim milk with the food processor or mixer running. Blend just until incorporated. Divide the mixture among the ramekins, then place them in a baking pan with sides. Pour hot water into the baking pan so that it comes halfway up the sides of the ramekins. Bake until set, about 35-40 minutes. Serve warm or let cool, then cover and refrigerate until ready to serve. Optional: dollop each ramekin with light whipped topping.

Serving size: 1 ramekin

Yields: 6 servings

Nutrition Facts (per serving): 154 calories, 4g total fat, 2g saturated fat, 89mg sodium, 25g carbohydrates, 3g fiber, *Gluten-Free*

Healthy Living Tip

Pumpkin is an excellent source of fiber which helps prevent cardiovascular disease, aids in weight management and promotes healthy digestion. A half cup of pumpkin contains 5 grams of fiber.

Maple Cream Cheese Pecan Squares

Crust

1/3 cup ground flaxseed

1/2 cup pecans

1/2 cup graham cracker crumbs

Filling

8 ounces 1/3 less fat cream cheese

8 ounces fat-free cream cheese

1 large omega-3 egg

1 1/2 teaspoons vanilla extract

2/3 cup sugar

1 3/4 cups chopped pecans

Topping

1 large egg

2 large egg whites

2/3 cup brown sugar firmly packed

1 1/2 teaspoons vanilla extract

1 1/4 cup sugar-free maple syrup (we like Log Cabin Sugar-Free)

Preheat oven to 350F degrees. Add flaxseed, 1/2 cup pecans, and graham cracker crumbs to blender or food processor and pulse into a crumb-like consistency. Press into a 9 x 13-inch dish. With an electric mixer beat the cream cheese, 1 whole egg, 2/3 cup sugar, and 1 1/2 teaspoons vanilla at medium speed until smooth. Spread the cream cheese mixture on top of the piecrust and sprinkle evenly with pecans. Whisk syrup, 1 whole egg, 2 egg whites, 2/3 cup brown sugar, and 1 1/2 teaspoons vanilla together and pour the mixture over the pecans. Bake for 50-55 minutes or until dessert is set. Cool on a wire rack for 1 hour or until completely cool. Serve immediately or cover and chill for up to 2 days.

Serving size: 1 square

Yields: 20 - 2 inch squares

Nutrition Facts (per serving): 168 calories, 10g total fat, 2g saturated fat, 163mg sodium, 16g carbohydrates, 2g fiber.

Healthy Living Tip

Milled (ground) flaxseed can be kept fresh for up to 30 days in a refrigerated, airtight container. Whole flaxseed can be stored in a dry place at room temperature for up to a year. To get the most nutritional value from flax, use a coffee grinder to freshly grind the seeds.

Peanut Butter Quinoa Cookies

1/2 cup honey

1/3 cup brown sugar

1/2 cup butter

1/2 cup natural peanut butter

1/2 teaspoon vanilla

1 cup rice flour

3/4 cup quinoa flakes

1 teaspoon baking soda

1/4 teaspoon salt

Heat the oven to 350F degrees. Beat the honey, brown sugar, butter, peanut butter, and vanilla in medium bowl until creamy. Combine the rice flour, quinoa flakes, baking soda and salt in a small bowl. Add to the mixture and beat until well-blended. Drop by rounded teaspoonfuls about 2 inches apart onto an ungreased cookie sheet. Bake for 12-15 minutes or until a light golden brown. Cool for 1 minute before removing from the cookie sheet.

Serving size: 1 cookie

Yields: 36 cookies

Nutrition Facts (per serving): 89 calories, 5g total fat, 2g saturated fat, 52mg sodium, 11g carbohydrates, <1g fiber, *Gluten-Free*

Healthy Living Tip

Everyone will like this gluten-free treat. Quinoa flakes are similar to oatmeal in texture and taste.

Pumpkin Mousse Tarts

15 ounces canned pumpkin

1/2 cup sugar-free prepared vanilla pudding

1 teaspoon pumpkin pie spice

1/4 cup Splenda

1 cup light whipped topping, 1/2 cup for mousse, 1/2 cup for topping tarts

45 frozen mini phyllo shells

1/2 teaspoon cinnamon

In a large bowl combine the pumpkin, pudding, spice and Splenda. Fold in 1/2 cup of the whipped topping. Put in a pastry bag or a zip-top plastic bag. Snip a ¼-inch hole in one bottom corner of the bag. Pipe into the phyllo shells and top with the remaining whipped topping, sprinkle with cinnamon.

Serving size: 1 tart

Yields: 45 tarts

Nutrition Facts (per serving): 20 calories, 1g total fat, 0g saturated fat, 20mg sodium, 4g carbohydrates, <1g fiber.

Healthy Living Tip

Pumpkin is a good source of potassium and magnesium which can help with blood pressure control. Refer to the DASH diet information in the Nutrition and Lifestyle Management section for other potassium and magnesium-rich foods.

Pumpkin Spice Cupcakes

Cupcakes

18.25 ounce box spice cake mix

1 cup canned pumpkin

1 cup unsweetened apple juice

1 cup Fuji apples, cored, peeled and diced

2 large eggs

2 egg whites

1 teaspoon vanilla extract

Frosting

1 8-ounce container frozen, fat-free whipped topping, thawed

2 teaspoons sugar

1/4 teaspoon ground allspice

1/2 teaspoon ground cinnamon

Preheat oven to 350F degrees. In large mixing bowl, stir the cupcake ingredients together. Using an electric mixer beat on low for 30 seconds, scraping the sides with a rubber spatula. Increase the speed to medium and beat for 2 minutes, scraping the sides. Spoon into two 12 cup muffin pans and bake for 20 minutes, or until a cake tester or toothpick inserted in the center of the muffins comes out clean. Let them cool on cooling racks for 15 minutes. Remove the cupcakes from the pans and let them cool completely. Meanwhile, put the whipped topping in a medium bowl and using a rubber spatula gently fold the sugar, allspice and cinnamon into the whipped topping. Cover and refrigerate until ready to use. When the cupcakes are completely cool, frost with the chilled topping.

Serving size: 1 cupcake

Yields: 24 cupcakes

Nutrition Facts (per serving): 106 calories, 2.5g total fat, 1g saturated fat, 180mg sodium, 19g carbohydrates, 1g fiber.

Healthy Living Tip

Pumpkin is a source of vitamin C and E which promote healthy skin.

Strawberry Parfaits

1 pint strawberries, sliced

¼ cup orange juice

1 tablespoon agave nectar

12 ounces light vanilla yogurt

1 cup balsamic vinegar

Wash the strawberries and remove the tops and slice. Marinate the strawberries in orange juice and agave nectar (you can use sugar substitute or sugar instead of agave nectar). Marinate for 30 minutes. In a clear glass cup, layer strawberry mixture, yogurt, then strawberry mixture. Repeat for remaining glasses. Drizzle with balsamic glaze.

Balsamic glaze: Place balsamic vinegar in a small saucepan and simmer until reduced to approximately ¼ cup. Allow to cool, then drizzle on top of parfaits. Store remaining balsamic glaze in the refrigerator for future use.

Serving size: 1 parfait

Yields: 4 servings

Nutrition Facts (per serving): 110 calories, 1g total fat, 0g saturated fat, 60mg sodium, 19g carbohydrates, 2g fiber, *Gluten-Free*

Healthy Living Tip

Agave nectar is a natural substitute for sugar. It tastes sweeter than sugar; therefore, you can use about 1/3 less. It is also lower on the glycemic index.

Summer Fruit Crisp

Filling

1/3 cup all-purpose flour

2 cans no-sugar-added sliced peaches, drained

2 cups strawberries, sliced

1/2 cup blueberries

1/4 cup Splenda Brown Sugar Blend

Topping

2 tablespoons all-purpose flour

1 tablespoon Splenda Brown Sugar Blend

3 tablespoons trans-free margarine

2 cups Honey Bunches of Oats with Almonds cereal, lightly crushed

1/4 cup flaxseed, ground

Preheat oven to 350F degrees.

For Filling: Combine the flour, fruit and Splenda. Place in an 8 x 8-inch baking dish.

For Topping: In a separate bowl, mix the flour, Splenda, and cut in margarine until mixture resembles wet sand. Add the cereal and flaxseed and stir well. Sprinkle over filling and bake for 25 minutes or until lightly browned.

Serving size: 1/2 cup

Yields: 8 servings

Nutrition Facts (per serving): 200 calories, 12g total fat, 5g saturated fat, 165mg sodium, 17g carbohydrates, 1g fiber.

Healthy Living Tip

Splenda Brown Sugar Blend is sweeter than regular brown sugar, thus half the amount is needed. Always check the conversion chart on Splenda Brown Sugar Blend package for your substitutions.

Surprise Meringues

2 extra large egg whites

1/8 teaspoon salt

1/8 teaspoon cream of tartar

1 teaspoon vanilla

3/4 cup sugar

1 6-ounce package semisweet chocolate chips

1/2 cup pecans, chopped

Preheat oven to 300F degrees. Place parchment paper on baking sheet. Beat egg whites, salt, cream of tartar, and vanilla until soft peaks are formed. Add sugar gradually, beating until stiff peaks form. Fold in chips and nuts, then drop the mixture by rounded spoonfuls on parchment paper. Bake for 25 minutes. Allow to cool on baking pan, then lift off. Tip: Don't make these too large or the filling will fall out of the cookie when you pick them up.

Serving size: 1 cookie

Yields: 20 cookies

Nutrition Facts (per serving): 90 calories, 4g total fat, 1.5g saturated fat, 22mg sodium, 13g carbohydrates, <1g fiber, *Gluten-Free*

Healthy Living Tip

The dark chocolate and nuts add healthy indulgence to this light meringue cookie.

Vanilla Apple Napoleon with Ice Cream

4 Fuji apples, cored, peeled and cut into eighths

½ cup apple cider

4 tablespoons agave nectar

1/2 vanilla bean, split and scraped

1 pinch nutmeg

8 phyllo pastry sheets

butter flavored cooking spray

low-fat ice cream, frozen yogurt or light whipped topping (optional)

Preheat oven to 350F degrees. Preheat a large sauté pan over medium-high heat. Coat the pan with cooking spray and sauté the apples until lightly browned. Add agave, cider, nutmeg and vanilla bean, then bring to a simmer. Transfer to baking dish and place in oven for 10-15 minutes or until soft but still holding their shape. Lay out one phyllo sheet and spray with cooking spray, repeat the process with three more sheets, stacking on top of each other. Set aside. Using the 4 remaining phyllo sheets, repeat the layering process. You will have two 4-layered sheet stacks. Cut each stack into 12 squares and bake on a sprayed cookie sheet until golden brown. Reserve. Build Napoleon's with three layers of phyllo and two layers of filling. Serve with low-fat ice cream, frozen yogurt, or light whipped topping, if desired.

Serving size: 1 Napoleon with 1/4 cup low-fat ice cream

Yields: 8 servings

Nutrition Facts (per serving): 196 calories, 3g total fat, <1g saturated fat, 125mg sodium, 39g carbohydrates, 2g fiber.

Miscellaneous

Featured: Harvest Pancakes and Superfood Smoothie

Garden Egg Scramble

1 tomato

1 jalapeno pepper

1/2 green pepper

1 cup fresh spinach

1 teaspoon olive oil

6 large omega-3 eggs

2 ounces reduced-fat cheddar cheese

1/4 teaspoon dried basil

salt and pepper to taste

Dice the tomato and peppers. In a large sauté pan heat olive oil, then add the peppers and tomatoes. Cook for about 5 minutes or until tender. In a bowl whisk the eggs. Add eggs, cheese, basil, salt and pepper to vegetable mixture. Scramble until done.

Serving size: 1/4 recipe

Yields: 4 servings

Nutrition Facts (per serving): 168 calories, 10g total fat, 3g saturated fat, 284mg sodium, 3g carbohydrates, 1g fiber, *Gluten-Free*

Healthy Living Tip

Omega-3 eggs have more omega-3 fatty acids due to the vegetarian diet fed to the hens. Other nutritional benefits for these eggs include 25% less saturated fat and more vitamin D, A, E, B-12, riboflavin and lutein than regular eggs. Eggs are a source of dietary cholesterol, but recent studies suggest eggs have no effect on blood cholesterol levels.

Harvest Pancakes

1/2 cup all-purpose flour	1/4 teaspoon nutmeg
1/2 cup whole wheat flour	3/4 cup low-fat buttermilk
1 teaspoon baking powder	1/2 cup canned pumpkin (or mashed sweet potato)
1/4 teaspoon baking soda	1/4 cup maple syrup
1/8 teaspoon salt	1 omega-3 egg
1 teaspoon cinnamon	1 tablespoon canola oil
1/4 teaspoon ginger	1/2 teaspoon vanilla

In a large mixing bowl add the flours, baking powder, cinnamon, ginger, nutmeg, baking soda, and salt. In another mixing bowl, whisk the buttermilk, pumpkin, maple syrup, egg, oil and vanilla together. Pour into the flour mixture, stirring until just moistened; the batter may be slightly lumpy. Add more buttermilk, if the pancake batter is too thick. Preheat a non-stick skillet over medium heat. Using a 1/4 cup measure, pour the batter onto the griddle to make the pancakes. Cook for 2 to 3 minutes, or until the tops are bubbly all over and the edges are dry.

For a healthy topping, mix 8 ounces of frozen fat-free whipped topping and 1/2 teaspoon of ground cinnamon. Dollop the topping mixture onto each pancake.

Serving size: 2 pancakes

Yields: 4 servings

Nutrition Facts (per serving): 245 calories, 4.5g total fat, <1g saturated fat, 301mg sodium, 44g carbohydrates, 4g fiber.

Healthy Living Tip

Compared to traditional pancakes this recipe has more fiber due to the whole wheat flour and pumpkin ingredients.

Superfood Smoothie

2 tablespoons ground flaxseed

1 cup light vanilla yogurt

1 1/2 cups frozen mixed berries

1 cup low-fat soy milk

1 banana

agave nectar or Splenda to taste

Place all ingredients in a blender and process until the desired texture is achieved. For a quick breakfast, measure the flaxseed, soymilk, yogurt and banana the night before and put it in a plastic food storage container in the refrigerator. In the morning, add the frozen fruit and combine the contents of the container into the blender.

Serving size: 1/4 recipe

Yields: 4 servings

Nutrition Facts (per serving): 160 calories, 3.5g total fat, <1g saturated fat, 77mg sodium, 28g carbohydrates, 4.5g fiber, ***Gluten-Free***

Healthy Living Tip

Why eat flaxseed? Flaxseed contains important nutrients: alpha linolenic acid (ALA), fiber and lignans. Alpha Linolenic Acid (ALA) is an essential type of omega-3 fatty acid. The body converts ALA to the omega-3 fatty acids found in fish (DHA and EPA). Benefits of fiber include digestive health and lowering blood cholesterol levels. Lignans are antioxidants found in flaxseed. Lignan content in flaxseed may protect against some cancers and lower blood cholesterol levels.

Trail Mix

1/2 cup Fiber One Cereal

1 cup Wheat Chex Cereal

1 cup pretzel sticks

1/4 cup roasted almonds

1/4 cup dried fruit

1/8 teaspoon cayenne pepper

1/4 teaspoon garlic powder

1/4 teaspoon Kosher salt

butter flavored cooking spray

Combine the Fiber One and Wheat Chex cereals with the pretzel sticks, almonds and fruit, then mix in the cayenne pepper, garlic powder and salt. Coat the mix with a butter flavored cooking spray. Spread on a baking pan and place in preheated 250F degree oven for 30 minutes, stirring twice during cooking time. Remove from oven to cool.

Serving size: 3/4 cup

Yields: 4 servings

Nutrition Facts (per serving): 168 calories, 4g fat, 1g saturated fat, 342mg sodium, 32g carbohydrates, 6g fiber.

Chocolate Snack Mix

1/2 cup Fiber One Cereal

1 cup Wheat Chex Cereal

1 cup pretzel sticks

1/4 cup roasted almonds

3 tablespoons semisweet chocolate chips

1/8 teaspoon cayenne pepper

butter flavored cooking spray

Combine the Fiber One and Wheat Chex cereals with the pretzel sticks, and almonds, then coat with butter flavored cooking spray. Spread on a baking pan and place in preheated 250F degree oven for 30 minutes, stirring twice during cooking time. Remove from oven to cool. In a microwave safe glass bowl add the chocolate and microwave it for 30 seconds, stir, and repeat until the chocolate is melted. Mix cayenne pepper in the melted chocolate. Drizzle chocolate over the cereal mixture.

Serving size: 3/4 cup

Yields: 4 servings

Nutrition Facts (per serving): 174 calories, 7g total fat, 2g saturated fat, 342mg sodium, 32g carbohydrates, 6g fiber.

Cucumber Water

2 quarts ice water   1 cucumber peeled, seeded and sliced

To flavor drinking water, add slices of cucumber instead of the usual lemon wedges. Place thin rounds in a pitcher of water and chill before serving. Garnish each glass with a cucumber round.

Serving size: 1 cup

Yields: 2 quarts

Nutrition Facts (per serving): 1 calories, 0g total fat, 0g saturated fat, 0mg sodium, <1g carbohydrates, 0g fiber, *Gluten-Free*

Healthy Living Tip

Drinking water throughout the day is not only necessary for proper hydration, but it can curb one's appetite and lead to weight management or weight loss. Cucumber adds a great natural, fresh, and cheap option to mix up the flavor of water.

Go Orange Splendor

2 quarts Crystal Light, Sunlight Classic Orange, prepared

1 quart Diet Sunkist Soda, chilled

2 oranges, sliced

2 lemons, sliced

In a punch bowl add prepared Crystal Light and Sunkist. Add sliced fruit placed in the beverage mixture. Chill for 2 hours. Serve over ice.

Serving size: 8 ounces

Yields: 12 servings

Nutrition Facts (per serving): 3 calories, 0g total fat, 0g saturated fat, 41mg sodium, 0g carbohydrates, 0g fiber, *Gluten-Free*

Hot Spiced Tea

8 cups water, divided

6 tea bags

1 1/4 cups Splenda, granular

4 cups orange juice

1/4 cup fresh lemon juice

4 cinnamon sticks

2 teaspoons whole cloves

Garnish: lemon slices and cinnamon sticks

In a large pot, bring 4 cups of water to a boil. Add tea bags and steep for 5 minutes. Stir in the Splenda, orange and lemon juices. In a small saucepan, combine 4 cups of water, cinnamon sticks and cloves, then bring to a boil, and simmer for 20 minutes. Pour spice mixture through a wire-mesh strainer into the tea mixture, discarding the spices. Serve tea hot with lemon slices and cinnamon sticks.

Serving size: 8 ounces

Yields: 12 servings

Nutrition Facts (per serving): 25 calories, 0g total fat, 0g saturated fat, 7mg sodium, 6g carbohydrates, *Gluten-Free*

Healthy Living Tip

Warm drinks can curb the appetite and aid in weight management. This recipe is low in calories and high in flavor. The hot spiced tea will fill your kitchen with wonderful holiday aromas too.

Iced Peach Green Tea

4 cups water

8 green tea bags

2 ripe peaches, pitted and sliced

2 cups cold water

1/2 cup Splenda

fresh mint leaves for garnish (optional)

Place peaches in a saucepan and add 4 cups of water, then heat until near a boil. Remove from heat, add the tea bags and steep for 5-6 minutes. Remove tea bags from the water, squeezing gently. Stir in 2 cups cold water and sweetener, stirring until sweetener dissolves. Allow the tea to cool, then refrigerate until thoroughly chilled. Serve over ice. Garnish with peach slice and mint sprig.

Serving size: 8 ounces

Yield: 8 servings

Nutrition Facts (per serving): 20 calories, 0g total fat, 0g saturated fat, 5mg sodium, 5g carbohydrates, <1g fiber, *Gluten-Free*

Healthy Living Tip

Green tea provides flavonoids, which work as antioxidants and may help protect the body against the damage created by free radicals.

Index

Gluten Free Recipe Index

Resources

The United States Department of Health and Human Services

The National Institutes of Health

The National Heart, Lung, and Blood Institute

- Dietary Approaches to Stop Hypertension
- National Cholesterol Education Program
- Therapeutic Lifestyle Change Diet
- Clinical Guidelines for the Identification, Evaluation, and Treatment of Obesity in Adults
- nhlbi.nih.gov

The United States Department of Agriculture

- Dietary Guidelines for Americans 2010
- National Nutrient Database for Standard Reference
- ChooseMyPlate.gov

The United States Food and Drug Administration

- Nutrition Facts Label
- usda.gov

Centers for Disease Control and Prevention

- Division of Nutrition, Physical Activity, and Obesity
- Physical Activity for Everyone: The Benefits of Physical Activity
- cdc.gov

The US National Library of Medicine

The National Institute of Health

- Medline Plus
- nlm.nih.gov/medlineplus/

American Heart Association

- americanheart.org

Academy of Nutrition and Dietetics

- eatright.org

American Diabetes Association

- diabetes.org

Celiac Disease Foundation

- celiac.org

American College of Sports Medicine

- acsm.org

Mayo Clinic Health Information

- mayoclinic.com